Dear Awesome Reader,

You are special and unique, and the world needs you very much.
The world lies waiting for your light to shine.
Now is the time.

Switch on!

Don't get distracted, diluted and confused by the external voices of people
who don't have any idea of the person you were born to be. You were born to win.

Switch on your personal power!

Switch On!

Veli Ndaba

ISBN 978-0-620-79505-0
Cover design by Dylan Fourie of Angry Monkey Creative Agency (Pty) Ltd (Springs)
Editing & proofreading by Eulália Snyman (Alberton)
Book design & layout by Dylan Fourie of Angry Monkey Creative Agency (Pty) Ltd (Springs)
Printed by - ActiveBrand
Photography by Maria Capazario of Photo Maria Studio (Pretoria) A South African publication

Endorsements

"I share the view that every one of us is born for a purpose. Our responsibility is to discover that purpose and completely fulfil it. Veli Ndaba wrote in his previous book, Your Dream is Calling You, that a tree never grows to half its intended size. He further wrote that the tree absorbs as much water and nutrients from the soil as it can, and grows to its full potential. And so, it should be with us human beings. The current book, is in my view, part of "the water and nutrients" available for us to absorb, as we strive to be the best we can be in fulfilling our respective purposes on this earth. The book, with key questions to ponder on at the end of each chapter, is a well written and an easy but impactful. I highly recommend this book to everyone, regardless of their stage in life, who wants to be the best they can be."
~ **Mr Lesibana Ledwaba**, executive at Barloworld, South Africa

"This is another meaningful instalment from amongst Veli's insightful and well-studied contributions to human understanding. Borrowing from his own life experiences, neuroscience and his work as a life coach, he uses this book to share rich insights on personal mastery, which will be beneficial to all that aspire to succeed in their lives."
~ Dr Bangani Ngeleza, strategic management practitioner; member of the Advisory Committee for the NECT Education Innovation Hub, South Africa

"Congratulations on your book. Interesting reading. The book leads into deep introspection "know yourself"... It questions the basis of our belief system, the foundation of our joy and brings in the impact of a strong mind with visualisation. Well done for this inspiring book."

~ **Dr Charles Ntwaza**, medical doctor, South Africa

"Switch On! is an important restorative book. Restorative in a sense that at its core structure, it deals with fundamental issues relating to making sense of complex events that shape our own personal worlds. This is particularly critical where, as individuals within the body of society, we are entrapped in a continuous cycle of unproductive routines and unhelpful behaviours, where much of the time as children, we may have grown up being moulded through a subtler process of invalidation.

This book sets itself apart as an instrument that assists with undoing how we have come to project ourselves as functioning human beings. It gives us as individuals, the tools to navigate the course of enlarging our area of identification by reclaiming previously suppressed, but positive aspects of our lives. It is through this approach that the book enables us to improve our capacity to entrench a positive belief system for ourselves to build confidence in ourselves to achieve our dreams – one dream at a time.

I am impressed with this book's practical action steps at the end of each topic. As a person who has spent time in academia, I appreciate the comprehensive nature of the book and very importantly, the useful 'Flip that Switch' section. Switch On!, as an easy to read and practical book provides a tool to help one chart a growth map towards self-betterment."
~ **Ms Conny Mametja**, local and public administration specialist, South Africa.

"I love this book! This book is not only inspiring, but also very empowering. It challenges your current beliefs and helps you unleash your personal power. When you are anchored in the power that created you, no storm has power over you. You may be shaken, but can never be dislodged."
~ **Mr Clifford Mohale Klaas**, executive director at Siemens South Africa.

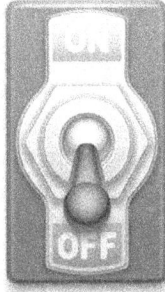

About Veli Ndaba

Veli Ndaba was born and bred in Soweto, South Africa. He studied management science at the University of South Africa, mechanical engineering at the University of Johannesburg and later embarked on a career in the corporate world.

Through hard work and dedication, he soon reached managerial level. However, he felt something was amiss. "I did not feel alive. It was as if something was suffocating me, and I knew I had to make a change. After all, if we do not move forward, life will just move on without us," he says.

In 2011, he started his own business, specialising in corporate training, life and business coaching. He joined communication and leadership organisation Toastmasters, eventually becoming president of his local club and mastering the art of public speaking. Today, Veli is living his dream.
He travels around South Africa giving motivational talks to people from all walks of life. He coaches individuals, conducts training at big corporations and inspires small and medium enterprises. 'Switch On!' is Veli's third book

Veli Ndaba lives in Alberton, a town situated about 20 km south east of Johannesburg. He is a family man; he is married to Mpumi and has two sons, Ntokozo and Sanele.

Contact Veli via email veli@velindaba.com or via LinkedIn. Instagram (Veli Ndaba), Twitter (Veli_Ndaba) and website www.velindaba.com All social media channels (FB, Twitter, Instagram and LinkedIn handle: @engineeredmindtowin)

Serenity Prayer

By Reinhold Niebuhr [1892 – 1971]

God grant me the serenity

to accept the things I cannot change; courage to change the

things I can; and wisdom to know the difference.

Living one day at a time; enjoying one moment at a time;

accepting hardships as the pathway to peace; taking, as He

did, this sinful world

as it is, not as I would have it; trusting that He will make all

things right

if I surrender to His Will;

that I may be reasonably happy in this life and supremely

happy with Him

forever in the next.

Amen.

Contents

Introduction

Getting started

"If you focus on success you'll have stress. But if you pursue excellence, success will be guaranteed."
– Deepak Chopra (1947 –), American author, public speaker and alternative medicine advocate

Hello and congratulations on investing in this book. I truly believe that it will make a difference in your life, especially if you read it over again every now and then. You see, in the battle between your thoughts and your habits, your habits always win and that is why you may need to re-read and refresh some of the information and tips that follow in the next few pages.

In fact, the reason why many people are frustrated with the results they produce is because their daily habits and thoughts are not in agreement with each other. You can work very hard – as most people do – but until your thoughts, dreams, beliefs and habits are in full agreement, your hard work will unfortunately be in vain.

Surely you must know someone who is clever, educated, smart and beautiful and yet hasn't achieved anything worth mention so far?
Maybe you are such a person. And you wonder how can this be that heaps of talent and intelligence and good looks haven't produced any remarkable results? The most probable explanation is that there's disagreement between your thoughts, dreams, beliefs and habits.

Let me use the analogy of a motor car: I am sure you'll agree with me that a motor car cannot go anywhere unless its four wheels are facing in the same direction. No matter how sleek, how aerodynamic or how powerful its engine, a car will go nowhere unless all wheels are aligned in the same direction, right? Furthermore, a car cannot drive itself to a desired destination; it needs a driver to switch it on. Even driverless cars need to be switched on. So, if you want to arrive at your dream destination in life, you have to ensure that your 'wheels' are aligned in the same direction. And you have to push the start button, you have to switch your engine on.

What are your 'wheels'? What is your 'engine' and how do you switch it on? These are things I write about in this book. My first book, 'You Are Born to Win', focuses mainly on getting you to believe in yourself. My second book, 'Your Dream is Calling You', reminds you that it isn't enough to believe in yourself – you need to have dreams. And now, with this book, I aim to help you align your thoughts, dreams, beliefs and habits – and start moving forward.

We all want to be switched on and to be moving forward, making progress in life. The problem is that we don't know how.

As our traditional school curriculum emphasises science, technology, engineering and mathematics, many of us don't know much about things that are critical in understanding how we human beings are wired. If you don't understand how your motor car works, how can you make use of all its features? The same applies to your quality of life; how can you live fully if you don't know yourself? If you don't understand yourself, how can you get started, never mind operate at optimum level?

Life is all about learning skills, using them to earn money and passing them on. That's how a legacy is created. It's said that success without successors is no success at all. I have spent time and effort studying people who have achieved great results in their lives. Success truly leaves clues and I am happy to report that I have benefited greatly from these clues and lessons.

I have written this book to share lessons, information and tips that have improved my life and I believe that they will do so for you too. The book sheds light on some of the things that will make it possible for you to unleash your greatness – things like joy, self-knowledge and harnessing the power of your mind. At the end of each chapter I've added a Flip that Switch section with clearly defined action steps that you can take immediately.

My goal is to inspire and empower people to realise their true potential and achieve their dreams. It is, however, important to note that greatness is not an automatic destination. Greatness only results from the good and deliberate quality choices that we make in our lives on a daily basis.

One quote that has been a major driving force in my life is by Henry David Thoreau and it goes as follows:
"I learned this, at least by my experiment that if one advances confidently in the direction of his dreams, and endeavours to live the life which he has imagined, he will meet with a success unexpected in common hours. He will put some things behind, will pass an invisible boundary; new, universal, and more liberal laws will begin to establish themselves around and within him; or the old laws be expanded, and interpreted in his favour in a more liberal sense, and he will live with the licence of a higher order of beings."

I invite you to read these words until you gain full understanding of them. It took me a while to fully submerge myself in the power of these words. I have had wonderful, unexpected experiences where I found myself saying, 'I can't believe that I am doing this.'

As a professional speaker and life coach, I get to meet and talk to a lot of people. Through my interactions with them, I get more or less the same reasons as to why they are not living their dreams and these reasons are the following:

- I am stuck and not happy where I am.
- I don't know what I am passionate about. If I did, I would be doing something about it.
- Can you really have a job that you love? Is a job not just a job?
- What will my friends and family think if I pursue something different?
- Who am I to think I can do something when I am lucky to even have a job?
- I have been a eacher/lawyer/accountant/engineer, etc. for so long, I don't have other skills!

If any of these sound familiar, don't worry because you're not alone. My aim is to help you get from where you are now – knowing you want something different, something more, but not exactly sure how to get there – to where you want (and deserve!) to be, namely doing work that excites you and living a life of joy.

I cannot claim to have all the answers to the big challenges and questions in life. But through the years I have learnt a couple of things that I'm delighted to share with you in this book so you can switch on your power and move towards a higher level of living and being.

Veli Ndaba
August 2018

It's good to be alive

"Our hearts ache, but we always have joy. We are poor, but we give spiritual riches to others. We own nothing, and yet we have everything."
St Paul (AD 5 – AD 67), apostle of Jesus Christ as quoted in the Holy Bible, 2 Corinthians 6:10

Joy is the starting point to unleashing your greatness. Yes, there are problems in the world and there will always be: wars, political instability, recession, earthquakes, tsunamis, drought,epidemics, plagues, unemployment, stock exchange crashes, corruption, crime, divorce, rebellion, genocide, discrimination, human trafficking, animal extinction, heat waves, cold snaps, floods, fires, accidents, terminal diseases, viruses and bacteria (remember bird flu, mad cow disease and listeriosis outbreaks?) among many others. You and I can't stop these things from happening. Yet, I bet you'll agree that it's good to be alive.

Despite the 'bad stuff' and challenges, it is awesome to experience life. It is so awesome, that it's worth the time and effort to try and experience life fully – the good and the bad. It is so awesome that sometimes we have joy in our hearts even when facing death.

You can't change the inevitability of death and you can't control what happens on the outside. That's the bad news. But you can, however, control how you deal with it. And that's the good news. If your belief about yourself and your ability to operate successfully in the world is positive, healthy, joyous and committed, nothing short of the end of the world can stop you. When you're in a positive frame of mind and have joy in your heart, it is easier to leave your comfort zone and switch on your power. Without joy and positivity you and I will get nowhere. It's the starting point to unleashing your greatness.

Let me point out that joy and happiness are often used interchangeably and yet there's a vast difference between them. I think it's quite important to understand the differences between the two in order to deal with life's ever-changing situations, events and failures.

Joy comes when you make peace with who you are, why you are and how you are. Happiness on the other hand tends to be externally triggered and is based on other people, things, places, thoughts and events. Joy is not an emotion, something that comes and goes, but an attitude of the heart. Happiness, on the other hand, is an emotion triggered by something outside of a person and is temporary.

When things get tough – as they inevitably do – you may be tempted to despair or express sadness and depression. You may think you have to choose between hardship and joy, or support and separation, or light and darkness. But consciousness is not an either/or equation. It's about 'bothness', writes Danielle La Porte in her blog (daniellelaporte.com). The famous American motivational speaker and author explains that the capacity to expand into 'bothness', the awareness of your joy in all circumstances is so much of what it means to evolve. This is succinctly expressed in the words of Agatha Christie which are as follows, "I like living. I have sometimes been wildly, despairingly, acutely miserable, wracked with sorrow, but through it all I still know quiet certainly that just to be alive is a grand thing."

"Happiness is like rising bubbles: delightful and inevitably passing. Joy is like oxygen, ever present. Happiness is always passing through. It can claim your full attention for the ten seconds it takes to swallow a sip of incredible coffee or beverage of your choice while joy can stream through for weeks on end," Danielle elaborates in her blog. "Joy is the fibre of your soul. It is the stuff of your essence. And since you, your soul, can never be crushed, your access to joy never vanishes. Because joy is so foundational to your true being, every other state or emotion can rest on top of joy, it can accommodate everything. This means that it's possible to grieve with your whole heart, and still sense your joy. You can feel rage, and be aware of joy waiting patiently for your return, and take deep comfort in that.

You can get fired, dumped and pulled through the eye of a needle, and still feel held by the container of joy – the truth of your existence. When you arrive at this awareness, your logical mind is going to be confused. This logical mind will say, "I'm going through hell. This is the worst thing that's ever happened to me... so what's this mighty warmth I feel within? I must be losing it. I must be in denial. I should get   back to misery." No, it won't be denial but a sign that you are expanding. When you see joy beside the agony, you have the keen vision of a soul warrior."

I love Danielle's words and I quote her because I think that nobody has said it better so far. I advise you to hold on to these words, "Since you, your soul, can never be crushed, your access to joy never vanishes." Put that sentence in your pocket and keep it for a rainy day, like the song says.

You always have access to joy, you just have to dig into your heart. You can never be crushed. The person who comes to mind as a perfect example of this is Dr Viktor Frankl who wrote the book 'Man's Search for Meaning' in 1946 shortly after leaving the Auschwitz concentration camp. He was an Austrian neurologist and psychiatrist as well as a Holocaust survivor. I recommend that you read his book. It's not very thick, but every page is packed with power and wisdom.

In short, Dr Frankl was Jewish and so the Nazis threw him into various concentration camps during World War II. All his family died except his sister, and he suffered terrible abuse at the hands of the Nazis.

As we know, not many people survived the Auschwitz concentration camp. But he did. Not only did he survive, but he went on to rebuild his life, marry again and live productively and joyfully until the ripe old age of 92. No wonder his book 'Man's Search for Meaning' is still a best seller to this day.

After enduring the suffering in the concentration camps, Frankl concluded that even in the most absurd, painful, and dehumanised situation, life has potential meaning and that, therefore, even suffering is meaningful.

He said, "What is to give light, must endure burning." At some point in the book he describes how he sucked for hours on a crumb of bread (the Nazis were not exactly generous, were they?) and was grateful to do so, because it meant he had food.

"We all said to each other in camp," he wrote, "that there could be no earthly happiness which could compensate for all we had suffered. But it was not the hope of happiness that gave us courage. It was the "will to meaning" that looked to the future, not to the past."

Much later (not in the book), Frankl wrote: "Again and again I therefore admonish my students in Europe and America: Don't aim at success - the more you aim at it and make it a target, the more you are going to miss it. For success, like happiness, cannot be pursued; it must ensue, and it only does so as the unintended side effect of one's personal dedication to a cause greater than oneself or as the by-product of one's surrender to a person other than oneself.

Happiness must happen, and the same holds for success: you have to let it happen by not caring about it. I want you to listen to what your conscience commands you to do and go on to carry it out to the best of your knowledge. Then you will live to see that   in the long-run – in the long-run, I say! – success will follow you precisely because you had forgotten to think about it."

Joyful people are typically content and serene. They don't necessarily smile and laugh a lot, but they have a positive outlook on life. They appreciate the small things in life (albeit a crumb of bread as in the case of Dr Frankl). They find it a great joy to be alive, to be here. If you won a lottery of R1 million, you'd be very happy, but if you work hard and earn R1 million, you will feel joy. Though the ultimate benefit is the same, the cause being different makes the final emotion different. Joy is long-lasting. It makes peace and happiness to be easily attainable in spite of one's circumstances and experiences.

One way to understand the difference between joy and happiness is to look at the opposites of the two. The opposite of joy is fear (and not sadness), while the opposite of happiness is unhappiness and misery. Joy warms a person's heart while happiness merely pleases. Happiness brings pleasure, but joy brings true contentment to one's heart.

Joy is not always about oneself; you can be joyful about another's well- being and happiness. Happiness is generally based on materialistic possessions and worldly pleasures and activities.

Joy comes from the depths of your soul and doesn't depend on your possessing anything material or on any activity. You can be in hospital, unable to move or talk and still find joy in being alive. While happiness comes from outside things, joy is about inner self. Joy leads to the serenity and peace which every human being craves.

In his Serenity Prayer (quoted in the front of this book), Reinhold Niebuhr shares five timeless truths that are important in the context of finding true joy. These are summarised on www.huffingtonpost.com as follows:

1.   Acceptance is not laziness.
When we devote inordinate attention to the things we cannot change, we expend physical, emotional and mental energy that could be directed elsewhere. Accepting that there are some things we cannot change does not make us complacent. It constitutes a leap of faith – an ability to trust, as the prayer goes on to say, "that He will make all things right if I surrender to His Will." We thus make the choice to let go and have faith in the outcome.

2.   We must have courage to change ourselves.
One of life's greatest challenges is imagining how our lives could be different than they are now. Often, our deeply-ingrained habits are our own worst enemies, and simply identifying them is half the battle won. Since habits gain power through repetition, it takes real focus and perspective to take a look at ourselves and our habits and ask, "Is this how I really want to live?" As the prayer states, this act of self-investigation is nothing less than an act of courage.

3. Hardship can be good for you.

As the prayer states, we must accept "hardships as the pathway to peace." Every person confronts obstacles in the course of his or her life. When we view these obstacles not just as frustrations or failures, but as opportunities for growth and learning, we can transcend our circumstances.

4. Surrendering requires courage, too.

The word 'surrender' has mostly negative connotations; we associate it with resignation, failure and weakness. But the Serenity Prayer reframes the notion of surrender as an act of faith and trust. The wisdom of the prayer lies in exchanging a life of endless "what ifs" for a life of trust in a power beyond ourselves, our Creator.

5. Happiness is attainable — now and in the future.

The prayer's ending has something very profound to say about happiness: if we follow the prayer's advice, we may be "reasonably happy in this life." Just reasonably? At a time when our culture measures happiness and success mostly in terms of money and power, that word "reasonably" stands out as an appealingly modest definition of a successful life. Rather than wondering why we aren't happier, orpicking through every minute aspect of our lives, the prayer asks us to focus on the present, "Living one day at a time" and "enjoying one moment at a time." Whether or not you believe in God or an afterlife, and whether or not the prayer's ending – a vision of being "supremely happy with Him forever in the next" – appeals to you or not, there's something universal in the prayer's quiet celebration of understanding our own potential, our own limits, and our capacity for transcendence.

Angus Buchan, a much-loved South African evangelist, recently wrote on the topic of joy against the background of a crippling drought in the Cape province, political and economic woes in the rest of South Africa. He wrote, "You can have joy during tough circumstances, sadness, difficulty or anything else. But you will not find joy if you are not living with purpose. Throughout history, countless men and women of God had purpose. The defining thing about their lives is the joy they had. You need to follow your dream and that will bring you joy. It will bring plenty of problems with it, for sure, but oh the joy! Money cannot buy you joy. When used as a tool to fulfil your Godly purpose, then money can be a blessing and bring great joy. Jesus is your joy- giver. He is the Prince of Peace who will flood your life with joy."

I urge you to sit alone in a quiet place and celebrate your existence, celebrate being alive. Dig for joy in your heart. The scariest thing for most people is to be alone, to come face-to-face with themselves. Many cannot go offline and switch off all the electronic devices around them. They have become slaves of these devices because they think that these bring happiness to them. Actually, these devices steal more happiness from you than you can imagine...but that's a topic for another day...

So, just take the time and go offline. Take a walk in the park and appreciate the beauty of nature, enjoy the chirping of birds and breathe in the fresh air. This will remind you of how blessed you are and it will rekindle the fire of joy burning in your heart. Feel free to blurt out loud: "Ah, indeed it is good to be alive!"

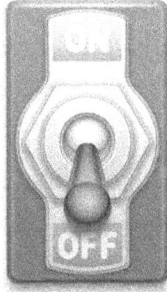

Flip that switch
Action Steps

> **Step 1**

Put your phone on silent and go for a short walk in a garden or a park. Sit down somewhere by yourself and read the following:

~Be grateful~
[as received on Whatsapp, author unknown]
The qualifications that gave you a job are the same as the qualifications that someone else has, but doesn't have a job...
Be grateful.
The prayer God answered for you is the same prayer others have been praying without success yet ...
Be grateful.
The road you use safely on a daily basis is the same road on which many others have died ...
Be grateful.
The place where you worship and God blessed you is the same place where others worship, but their lives are still in shambles
...
Be grateful.

The bed you used in the hospital before you got healed and discharged, is the same bed where upon other people have died...

Be grateful.
The same rain that made your field produce good crops is the same rain that destroyed someone else's field ...
Be grateful.
Be grateful because whatever you have is not by your own power, might or qualifications, but rather by the Grace of the Almighty God, the giver of life.

➢ **Step 2**
Write a text to yourself saying it is good to be alive because ... and give 5 reasons. Send the message to yourself (you can SMS or Whatsapp). Read the message out loud. Smile. Take a deep breath. Exhale. Repeat five times.

➢ **Step 3**
Go back to what you were doing previously or move on to your next task.

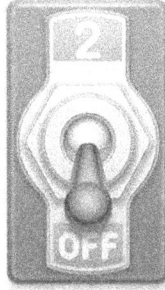

Know yourself

"Man, know thyself; then thou shalt know the universe and God."
– Pythagoras (570 BC – 495 BC), Greek mathematician and philosopher

We all have talents and abilities, but many of us don't bother to develop them. This can be because we're not aware of such talents. It can also be because of our conditioning and circumstances and because we're surrounded by people who don't inspire us to bring out our greatness. And so we settle for mediocrity. We don't dare to dream.

Do you really want more or are you satisfied? For me to change and claim my greatness, it was because I had gotten to a point where I wanted more in life.

I had become sick and tired of being sick tired of the situation I was in. This simply meant I had to think and behave differently in order for me to generate different results. I knew I deserved better, but I didn't know how I could do better. I was blinded by the circumstances and events in my life. I was restricted by my limited thinking; I really couldn't see beyond where I was. I didn't really know myself well enough to realise that I was capable of more.

I didn't think it was possible that I could earn a living from speaking and motivating people. I worried about my flaws as a person and therefore talked myself out of changing careers. For years and years, I also listened to voices
of well-meaning people who told me I was well placed where I was, and I had huge potential to become an executive manager in my line of work. They advised me to work hard and study further to stand a chance to get to the top of the organisation. This is part of what I call common consciousness – work hard and study further and you will achieve your dreams. Fortunately, I eventually learnt that you must not let your voice be drowned by external voices and common consciousness. You are the only one who knows the desires of your heart. And you're the only one that has the responsibility to make those desires and dreams come true.

My advice to you – if you want to make your dreams come true – it is for you to invest time discovering who you really are. Get to know yourself well.

Who are you? What makes you different to another? Get down to the nitty-gritty details of yourself. What makes you angry? What excites you? What bores you? Are you a morning person or night person? How much sleep do you need to operate at your best? What food isn't good for you? We are definitely not all the same; some people need four hours sleep per night while others need eight. Some people are lactose intolerant while others can drink litres of milk. Where do you fit in? What are your specifications? Most of us know our mobile phone specs better than we know our own personal specs.

Then, once you know yourself, learn to accept yourself for who you are. Learn to love yourself. I know it's easier said than done, but knowledge and love of self is essential. How can you be motivated to switch on your power when you don't like yourself? And how can you start unleashing your greatness when you don't know what your greatness is? Bear in mind that what you regard as being greatness, may be insanity in someone else's opinion, by the way.

I find that there is fun and joy in the process of discovering our true selves. Don't hesitate to have a good laugh or two at yourself. And don't hesitate to be creative in finding the true you. For example, you can pretend you're someone famous and interview yourself! Ask yourself difficult questions. American author, entrepreneur, philanthropist and life coach Anthony Robbins says that, "Successful people ask better questions, and as a result, they get better answers." If you learn to ask good quality questions, you will be forced to formulate good quality answers too.

Are you going to go through life with little dreams unworthy of serious discussion? Something I notice about people everywhere I go is that they mainly talk about the latest sporting event and what is going on in the news. I seldom hear people talking about themselves and their dreams. However, it's good to ask other people about how they see you, as this can give you a different perspective. It's also good to tell others about your dreams so they know where you are headed. We have been socialised to think that talking about yourself is a no-no. The truth about life is that it's in your hands. You were born with gifts and talents and it is up to you whether you will exploit or squander them; the choice is yours.

In my coaching work, one of my favourite questions is, "Why are you studying further? The different answers I get clearly show that most people study further because it is a job requirement. This means most people study further to meet the next position's specification or requirement; they don't study so as to become the best in what they do nor do they study to become better versions of themselves. I find this approach or thinking lacking proper reasoning. This to me signals that we don't know who we are, we don't understand ourselves.

To claim your rightful place in life, you have to give up who you have been for who you can become, you can't be both. Giving up who you have been will make way for your dreams, talents and abilities that have always been lying dormant within you.

As you begin this journey of unleashing your greatness, you have to let some people go. Many people never achieve their goals because they have surrounded themselves with too many negative, toxic and energy draining people. These people always find fault with you and make you doubt yourself whenever you want to do something. They want you to keep them company in their mediocre lives. These people will short circuit your potential for greatness.

There is no way you can soar like an eagle when you are surrounded with pigeons. This is what you have to come to terms with or else you will be stuck where you are. This is a critical step of detoxing and upgrading your relationships. Surround yourself with people that you can learn from because there's power in association.

I have no idea who wrote the following words that someone sent to me via Whatsapp, but and I think that it's quite sharp:

Never put temporary people in the permanent place of your life, and don't be afraid of removing the wrong people from the right place of your life. If it's your life, then it's your right.
Be bold to take any decision concerning your life, and if they call it pride, tell them it's class.
No matter the economy of the jungle, lions never eat grass, and even if education is free, a rat will never go to the same school as a cat. Avoid negative people because they are like cars without fuel; they have comfortable seats, but they can't take you anywhere.

When I wanted to be a professional speaker, I surrounded myself with world class people who were ahead of me. I joined Toastmasters International, read books, watched videos of the masters, and attended workshops, seminars and conferences to learn from the masters and also to meet like-minded people. I visualised being on stage like them. It is through these interactions and meetings that you can upgrade your relationships.

It's a known fact that we all have 24-hour days, 365 days a year, equal number of seasons in a year and face similar life challenges that may differ slightly from country to country. The main difference is how we set our priorities. Let's say two people have the same list of 10 possible activities to do. If they were to choose three same activities as their top priorities out of the ten, the first person may choose activities A, B, C as the 1st, 2nd and 3rd respectively while the activities A, B, C may be priorities 8th, 9th and 10th respectively on the second person's list. This, without a doubt, will have a significant difference in the results produced.

Someone may choose to watch television for three hours while the other chooses to read an inspirational book for the same number of hours. Also, one may choose to play games on his cell phone for about two hours while the other spends two hours watching and learning about a particular subject from YouTube videos. Without a doubt, these two people had the same amount of time but prioritised their activities differently in that time, hence the results will be different.

People that have a larger vision of themselves are serious about taking their lives to the next level. That larger vision is fuelled by listening and reading, taking in new information that gives them mental capacity to live out of their imagination as opposed to their memory. This new information challenges them and stimulates their imagination. Imagination is important. Albert Einstein explained that imagination is the preview of that which is to come. So get to know who you are and how great you are – and then imagine how much greater you can become. Jim Rohn, author of 'The Art of Exceptional Living' said, "When the end comes for you, let it find you conquering a new mountain, not sliding down an old one."

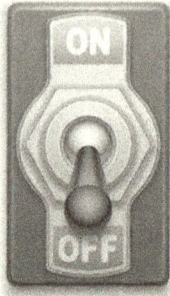

Flip that switch
Action Steps

> **Step 1**

Ask yourself the following questions and write down your answers:

1. What is it that you are supposed to do with this life of yours? Someone once said that our lives are a gift from God and how we live them is our gift to God. Would you honestly say that how you live your life is   the best gift you can ever give to your Maker? Have you thought about this seriously? If you had to be who you are today for the rest of your life, would you be satisfied? What areas of your life would you change?

2. What would you have to change, or become, or acquire in order to do what you are supposed to do with this precious life of yours? What areas of your life would you change? This may be in your health, relationships, career, business or something you want to do for the community before you die.

3. Are you willing to do whatever is required in order to do what you need to do? This is about resolve and commitment. Are you really willing to commit to your commitment? Horace Mann said, "Be ashamed to die until you have won some victory for humanity."

These questions will help you clarify your thoughts about what you need to do. They will shift you from being a jack of all trades and a master of none and become a force to be reckoned with in your chosen field.

➢ Step 2
Interview yourself or ask someone to interview you:
1. Who are you?
2. What makes you different to another person?
3. What makes you angry?
4. What excites you?
5. What bores you?
6. Are you a morning person or night person?
7. How much sleep do you need to operate at your best?
8. What food isn't good for you?
9. What are your specs? height / weight / gender / talents / abilities
10. What is your life's purpose?
11. What are the three things you'd like to achieve in the short term (3-5 years)?
12. What are the three things you'd like to achieve in the long term (5 years and longer)?
13. What are your pet hates?
14. What is your favourite colour?
15. What is your favourite song?
16. What is your favourite animal?
17. What is your favourite saying?
18. What is your favourite book?

19. What person/s do you admire the most and why?
Add more questions & answers here:

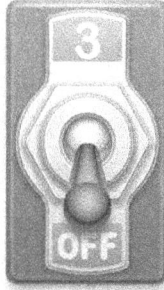

Beliefs

"People become really quite remarkable when they start thinking that they can do things. When they believe in themselves they have the first secret of success."
– Norman Vincent Peale (1898 – 1993), American pastor and author of best-selling 'The Power of Positive Thinking'

Many people are completely oblivious to the power of their beliefs. Yet, beliefs carry emotion, and emotion turns to action. That then influences the way we live. Whether you hold negative or positive beliefs about relationships, finances or your own abilities — they all carve out the path that is your life.

A belief is a feeling of certainty about something. It's not necessarily the absolute truth about something. This is because any truth always has three elements to it: a) your impression of the truth; b) another person's impression of the truth and then c) the factual truth, which is often quite different from the other 'truths'.

Why should we spend time talking about beliefs if beliefs don't necessarily reflect true facts? Because beliefs are the thoughts in our heads that shape our behaviour, attitude and actions. We have beliefs for every part of life, among others religious beliefs, financial beliefs, health beliefs and relationship beliefs.

The beliefs that affect our lives are either empowering beliefs which enable us to lead flourishing lives or self-limiting beliefs that stop us from achieving our goals, causing us to languish and struggle.

I once read an article about how Lucas Radebe almost ran away from football greatness. In the article he describes how in the early days of his international career, he had his bags packed, an airline ticket in his pocket and was ready to secretly escape from Leeds, (England) and fly back to Johannesburg.

Radebe's first few months in the north of England were tough and he hated the place. "Going overseas for me was like walking into a dark room blindfolded. I had no idea what to expect, I didn't know anything about Leeds United - and when I arrived it was horrible, I hated it," he said. To make matters worse, he had only made a few appearances for the team – as a substitute.

By the end of the year (December 1994), Radebe was thoroughly depressed. It was Christmas and he was homesick. That is when he packed his bags and decided to go home. But as he was about to open the door and leave the apartment where he was staying, he changed his mind. "Standing there, I realised the opportunity I had, and the responsibility I had, of not just representing myself but also my country and of the chance to open some doors for other African players," he explained to the journalist.

So he stayed in England to pursue his dream and the rest is history. He became a personal friend of Nelson Mandela, a FIFA ambassador, one of Leeds United's finest players of modern times and a much-loved South African sportsman.

Lucas Radebe is a great example of how we must not give up when times are tough. His story illustrates how important it is to believe in yourself and persevere. You can read the article written by Mike Collett at https://www.sowetanlive.co.za/sport/2010-10-05-how-lucas-radebe-almost-ran-away- from-football-greatness. You can also read his autobiography, called 'From the Streets of Soweto to Soccer Superstar' in which he tells how he went from being a Soweto hoodlum who stole and hijacked cars, to a successful professional footballer.

Let's look at some common self-limiting beliefs that we are used to hearing.

1. All the good ones are taken
2. You have to have money to make money
3. I have already tried everything
4. I am too old to change now
5. It's too late to start now
6. I'll never get that promotion

7. I have never been able to manage my time well

The problem with self-limiting beliefs is that they can be so sneaky. Quite often we aren't even aware that these little negative ideas are lurking in the shadows. Also notice how many of them are clichés. These are phrases we've heard for so many years, we don't even question whether they are true, or if there might be some underlying negative meaning.

Nothing in this world is so elusive yet so powerful as our beliefs. They have the power to dictate the direction of our lives, for good or bad, and they seemingly come out of nowhere. But where do your beliefs really come from? Simply put, they are developed as a
child and stick with you into adulthood. A belief is formed as a result of four main things:

1. Environment
2. events,
3. role models and
4. peer influence.

Think of it as a table with four legs (environment, events, role models and peer influence), as Guy Reichard, life and executive coach suggests on his blog, 'Dissolving Limits. Expanding Possibilities!' at
www.coachingbreakthroughs.ca/theblog/

Beliefs

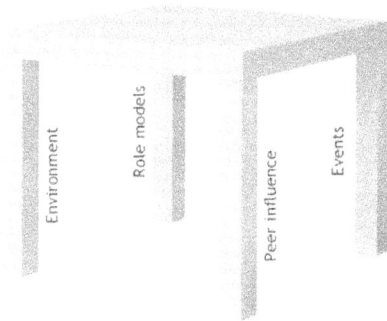

Brain studies have proven that childhood experiences make a lasting imprint on the subconscious mind. That includes things that we witness or hear about, people and circumstances that we encounter, and everything we are told by others.

All of that becomes so deeply ingrained that even when we aren't aware of it, those deep impressions have a strong influence over us for the rest of our lives. That can be good news or bad news.

There are valuable learning experiences that serve us well, but then there are also influences that keep us stuck and unable to move forward through life.
We all experience negative thoughts and moments of doubting ourselves, and we may sometimes face situations that make us feel afraid.
That's to be expected on occasion. The problem occurs when we are being subconsciously driven by these unwanted thoughts and emotions.

They are in control, and we don't even realise it. How do you take back your life? You have to learn to let go of the beliefs that keep holding you back.   If you're ever going to move forward in your life, you first have to figure out exactly what kinds of early life experiences are still having an adverse effect on you as an adult. That's not as simple as it sounds, so let's start with a few basic examples.

The first thing is fear. What kid has never felt afraid?! Growing up is pretty scary. What if you fail your test? What if the other kids laugh at something you say or the clothes you're wearing? What if nobody asks you to the big school dance? What if you ask that cute girl and she says no? Unfortunately, some of the things we feared as children actually happened. There were times that kids did make fun of you, or you tried your best but still failed an exam, or you got your feelings hurt and your heart broken.

Whether it was failing at something or feeling humiliated, your fears were validated. Worse, your brain then filed that away as "proof" that you should be afraid. As an adult you wear that fear like a bullet-proof vest, and it prevents you from ever taking any risk or even from stepping slightly outside of your comfort zone.

Procrastination is the second thing. Quite often, procrastination works just fine for kids. You can mow the lawn, or you can go play ball with your friends. For a child that choice is a no-brainer. Of course, the pay-off is only short-lived, and you'll probably get shouted at, but it's worth it. You know the consequences, but in a child's mind it's not too hard to shove them aside in favour of living for the moment.

Doing that often enough makes it easier and easier to dismiss the consequences of your own actions. You develop a habit that, over time, becomes addictive. The problem with bringing that into adulthood is that you've got a lot more on the line. Procrastination can have devastating effects on just about every aspect of your life, from your relationships to your career to your finances.

The third thing is self-doubt. Even if you had the best parents in the world, chances are you got a little damaged growing up. Their intent was to protect and to teach you, but from your standpoint it felt more like being constantly examined, judged, and criticised: "Stop that. Don't touch that! How many times do I have to tell you? Shame on you. What will people think?! I told you so. You should have known better. What were you thinking?!"

This isn't about blaming your parents. It's about understanding what you internalised as a child that no longer serves you. As an adult, no one is in charge of you but you. Only you have the right to criticise you. The problem is that those echoes from the past are still loud and clear in your head. You don't realise where all those put-downs are coming from, and you don't think to question it because your brain has accepted them as fact. When such a negative thought arises, you believe it is true.

Those are just three examples of childhood experiences that can be damaging. One other, and perhaps most important, is living a passionless life. The fortunate few discover a skill or talent in childhood and turn it into a fulfilling and successful career.

More often though, we either never have an opportunity to explore any paths that bring us joy, or we lose sight of them under the day-to-day pressures of making a living. Instead of seeking out what would fulfil us on a deeper level, we end up settling for whatever comes up. We live by default, because we have given up.

If any of the above strikes a chord in you, then you may think you've got it all figured out. Maybe, but it's easy to be deceived. Remember that we're talking about what's going on in your subconscious mind, so the answers aren't always straightforward. You may not know yourself quite as well as you think. You might even reach a conclusion when in fact, the truth is pretty much the opposite.

Sometimes you need to change a certain belief to let it collapse into oblivion. See the belief as a table top that has legs that are keeping it up. To collapse the table, you have to chop off its legs, one at a time:

> **Step 1:** Identify your belief (represented by the table top)
> **Step 2:** Isolate the reasons (represented by the legs) that hold the belief
> **Step 3:** Attack the reasons with logic; (attack the legs NOT the table top)

The legs of the table are the reasons that hold the belief up. Belief is the table top. The secret here is to attack the legs NOT the table top. The legs can be identified by asking these two questions:

1. 'That's an interesting belief I/you have…What are the reasons you have to believe that?'
2. Why do you say that? The reasons will then be provided and that's what you need to deal with.

Richard Petrie who wrote the book 'The Secret to Changing Subconscious Belief', used a fantastic example to clarify this. Belief: Muhammad Ali is the greatest boxer of all time.

Reason (Leg) 1: He was named the sportsman of the century. The counter argument to this reason is – who named him as the sportsman of the century and the answer is the journalists. The journalists are not the best judges, they may have been biased in the first place.

Reason (Leg) 2: He had a record of 56 wins – 5 losses.

He also beat George Forman and Joe Frazier. The counter argument - Rocky Marciano had a record of 49-0, so this record does not qualify Muhammad Ali to be the greatest boxer of all time.

Reason (Leg) 3: He won a gold medal in Rome. The counter argument: many people have achieved that.

Take a belief like, "Porsche is the best car ever designed". Now you canisolate the legs of the table (beliefs) as in Muhammad Ali's example. You don't necessarily need to attack all three or above legs of the table, with one leg or two, the table (belief) collapses. This is how I deal with some common beliefs in my life and this approach has helped me change my life in an amazing way.

Don't be held back by self-limiting beliefs. Use the table approach and change your life for the better. It's worth it; you are worth it.

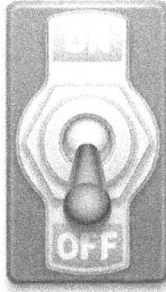

Flip that switch

Action Steps

➢ **Step 1**

Your beliefs are the coloured glasses through which you see the world. You interpret everything around you through those lenses. If I told you that you were beautiful, you could agree (if you believed yourself to be beautiful) or think I was crazy (if you believed yourself to be ugly).

But if I told you that your skin was purple, it's highly likely that you'd think that I was simply crazy because you know that your skin isn't purple.

So, in what areas of your life are your beliefs holding you back? Think about it

➢ **Step 2**

Write down what beliefs are holding you back from reaching your peak:

Mentally:

Emotionally:

Financially:

Physically

Relationships:

Spiritually:

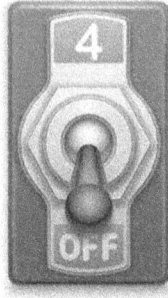

The amazing power of your mind

"Few people think more than two or three times a year: I have made an international reputation for myself by thinking once or twice a week."
– George Bernard Shaw (1856 – 1950), Irish playwright and winner of the Nobel Prize for Literature in 1925

One of the greatest resources you have is the supercomputer between your ears: your mind.
Therefore, one of the best investments you can ever make is to hone your thinking ability and learn about how your mind works.

Just think about physical fitness. Many people are aware that physical fitness is important, and they allocate time to exercise. But what about mind fitness? How many people allocate time to exercise their mind? Not many I'm afraid. But as George Bernard Shaw said in the quote above, the few who do so, are likely to surpass other people and achieve great things.

Let's compare your mind to the most sophisticated man-made device ever created, the computer. The average computer can hold about 250k pictures, 20k songs and hundreds of full length videos (movies). Nowadays this can be contained in something about the size of a pinkie finger and even less, unbelievable.

Average Computer

❖ 250k pictures;
❖ 20k songs;
❖ 100s full length videos (movies)

Human Mind

❖ Performs 10 Quadrillion
   (1k trill ^15) ops/sec;
❖ Blood flow throughout your veins
   with correct pressure
❖ Controls your heart beat,
   body core temperature
❖ Performs 6 trillion actions to about
   60 trillion cells every second

Now let's compare it to your mind: your mind can perform an estimated 10 quadrillion (1k trillion - 10 power 15) operations per second without you even knowing about it. Ask yourself right now, what's making your blood flow through out your veins with the perfect amount of pressure to keep you alive? What's making your heart beat right now? Are you consciously commanding your heart to beat right now? No.

What is maintaining your body core temperature to the perfect degree to keep you alive? What's performing six trillion essential actions to your 60 trillion cells every single second? It's something called your subconscious mind. This is the powerhouse that determines your life. There is only one thing that your subconscious mind cannot do and that is it can't distinguish between a real event and something you merely think about.

What happens when you have a nightmare? You wake up and your heart is pounding, you're anxious beyond words. The nightmare existed in your mind, you weren't in any real danger at all but, your mind didn't know that. You physiologically reacted as if the nightmare was taking place in reality.

I've read about a study during which a doctor hooked up an elite athlete, a professional skier, to a device that tested the athlete's muscle fibres. The doctor told the skier to merely think about skiing down a hill without making a single movement with his body. The act of thinking about skiing activated the muscle fibres (that would have performed when skiing) though the athlete was standing still.

The so-called placebo effect also demonstrates the power of the subconscious mind: a group of people suffering from a particular illness gets prescribed an approved drug specifically designed to treat that illness, another group of people suffering from the same illness gets a sugar pill (placebo) thinking it's real medication. End result?

Both groups get cured. Researchers suspect that about one third of all medical treatment, including surgery, is due to the belief that the treatment is going to work. There's also something called the nocebo effect – it's practically the opposite of the placebo effect. The mind, instead of curing illness, contributes to illness. The bottom-line is that the beliefs you hold in your subconscious mind become your reality.

Whatever we hold predominantly in the back of our subconscious minds we are attracted to in life, this is the RAS (Reticular Activating System) at play. What happens when you buy a new car? Suddenly you start to see a lot of cars of the same make everywhere you go. Why didn't you notice these cars previously? It's because you previously didn't own and didn't think about that make of car. What you hold in your mind you're attracted to in life.

If what you hold in your subconscious mind shapes your reality, what shapes your subconscious mind? Practically everything that you are exposed to, everything that you see, hear, smell, taste and feel (five physical senses) is shaping your subconscious mind. TV, radio, Xbox games. Choose what you watch and listen to.

Avoid holding negative thoughts in your mind because when that happens, the biochemistry of your brain changes and your body releases cortisol, the stress hormone, into your blood. Cortisol weakens your immune system, inhibits the actions of your white blood cells and increase the chances of infection and even promotes weight gain.

Be careful of the thoughts your mind dwells on. We average about 60 000 thoughts a day and the reality is most of these thoughts are the same thoughts we have day in and day out. If the thoughts are negative, your body automatically releases cortisol into your blood stream – without you being aware of it.

Most people believe that situations cause anxiety, stress and depression in our lives. Wrong! The reality is that there's no situation that can cause someone to experience anxiety or depression. It's your psychological reaction to the situation that can cause you to experience anxiety, not the situation itself – this is crucial to understand. Why is it that when some people skydive, their brains release endorphins (the feel-good hormone) while others release cortisol (the stress hormone)? It's because it's never the situation that causes anyone to experience anxiety, but their reaction to it.

Your situation doesn't control your anxiety. You control your anxiety. When you truly understand this truth, that's when you realise that you are in control of your life (well, mostly). It's one of the most liberating truths in life. You can create and you can take away anxiety, stress and depression in most cases (some cases you need medication) when you know what your subconscious mind is doing and you control it.

Even though society places great emphasis on our five senses (our ability to see, hear, smell, taste and touch) as the ways to perceive our world, we are the most powerful when we use and develop the six mental faculties we all possess:
1. Reason
2. Memory
3. Perception
4. Intuition

5. Will
6. Imagination

Each of these higher faculties of the subconscious mind are a kind of super power we can use to create a life we love.

Mental faculties are, as the name suggests, the instruments by and through which the mind performs various functions and tasks. It may come as a surprise to some, but observations indicate that these faculties are not exclusive to any individual or group of individuals. Rather, they are possessed by each and every person.

However, the possession of any faculty – mental or other – means little or nothing, if a person is unaware of their existence, or lacks the knowledge of how to best employ these faculties. It is not my intent to delve deeply into the intricate details of how the human mind works, but rather to give brief insight into the six mental faculties.

1. Reason

The dictionary-based definition of 'reason' is to form conclusions, judgments, or inferences from facts or premises. We're constantly exposed to heaps of information from numerous sources. We employ the mental faculty of reasoning as a filter to choose the information that will reside in our conscious mind.

The subconscious mind operates by deductive reasoning, whereas the conscious mind operates with both deductive reasoning as well as what is called inductive reasoning.

Inductive reasoning is looking for a pattern or trend from given information and then generalises it or makes a prediction out of it. So, I can safely say that it extrapolates information based on the known information and forecast or predict the future information out of it. Let's say someone wants to estimate the population of a particular town in upcoming years. If the past population numbers of this town is known, say for 1970, 1980, 1990, 2000 and 2010. One can use this information to predict the population in 2020 and 2030. This information can only be estimated by using forecasting. Inductive reasoning is used in these kinds of situations where the known past is used to predict the unknown future.

Deductive reasoning on the other hand entails taking a set of factual information and using it to deduce other facts that are also true. With this type of reasoning, you don't generalise or assume but you use facts. It starts with an argument or hypothesis and ends with a specific conclusion, for example: Mpumi is an aunt. It follows that she is woman and has a sibling.

Reasoning gives us the ability to think, to be consciously aware of the thoughts and ideas that come to our mind, and to reject or accept them into our reality. This is undoubtedly one of the most precious gifts God gave us: the ability to choose what images we hold in our minds and create our results.

Our mental faculty to reason acts like a cool screenplay writer providing a few possible alternate endings and we are the savvy directors choosing what makes the cut. Reason analyses, compares, and evaluates ideas, and it helps us choose wisely. Neuroscience has shown that the conscious mind only uses about 5% of the brain. Our mind is one of the best tools we have to access infinite wisdom, and when we do use it we set ourselves for success.

2. Memory

Memory is one of the most important cognitive components of our mind. The memory process is a collection of three sub-processes, namely encoding, storing, retrieval.

I think it's obvious what each one does. Encoding is the initial process when the mind perceives and registers the information. Storing is to keep the encoded information in a good shape so to be remembered easily over the time. And lastly the retrieval process recovers the stored information on the individual's demand.

There are three basic memory types, namely sensory, short-term or working memory and long-term memory.
Sensory refers to the initial process of storing information that is perceived through our senses. It lasts for a subtle period and it is regularly replaced by new data, as our senses work continuously.

Sensory memory is divided into five memory types, one per each sense. Let's suppose that you browse through a magazine very quickly.
You are most probably unable to remember anything in particular, not a whole page, a headline or a picture. As your eyes scan the magazine's pages, your mind is registering fast and briefly the incoming information. While you continue doing this, your mind receives new information and replaces the old one. This type of sensory memory is called iconic and lasts for about one second. Then, the data gets replaced by new sensory data.

This memory type relates not only to vision, but all the human senses. Echoic (hearing) type for example operates just like the iconic, but it lasts a little longer, about four seconds. As you look at the magazine, something may get your attention. While you stay on the page longer to read it properly, the short-term or working memory is activated.

Short-term or working memory is the ability to store information for a short time. We can hold information in the working memory by repetition. A classic example is when you need to remember a phone number until you find a piece of paper to write it down; you are repeating it to yourself. If something distracts you, then you can easily forget the number.

A general characteristic of working memory is that you won't remember after a short period. Another aspect of the working memory is that it has a limited capacity. Various tests can prove it. The most common test is to draw up a long list of items and then try to remember as many listed items as possible.

The capacity of the working memory type is about seven items at a time. This memory type seems to be closely correlated with intelligence; the higher the capacity of the working memory, the more intelligent the individual.

Long-term memory points to the ability to remember things for a very long time or the entire lifespan. Memories such as the movie you watched yesterday, playing basketball, academic or encyclopaedic knowledge and the date that you got your degree, are all set in the long-term memory.

In contrast with the two previous memory types, this type has no capacity limitations. You can get unlimited new knowledge and skills throughout your life. It is believed that when you train your brain by acquiring new knowledge and abilities, you slow down the brain's ageing process.

Most of us can take advantage of brain plasticity to improve our capacity to memorise and store information, and remember it when we need it. We can also use memory to create a better future for ourselves.

In the book 'Alice in Wonderland', the Red Queen asks Alice, "Tell me what you did tomorrow?"
Alice answers, "Well that is impossible, nobody can tell you what they did tomorrow. Tomorrow hasn't happened yet."
The Queen says to Alice, "Well, it's a pretty poor memory that only works in one direction."

That dialogue makes you think, doesn't it? I actually write myself letters from the future, telling myself what I did tomorrow. I can attest that something I commit to my memory has become true and also, that holding on to tragic memories has held me back from succeeding many times. How are you using your memory to create your success?

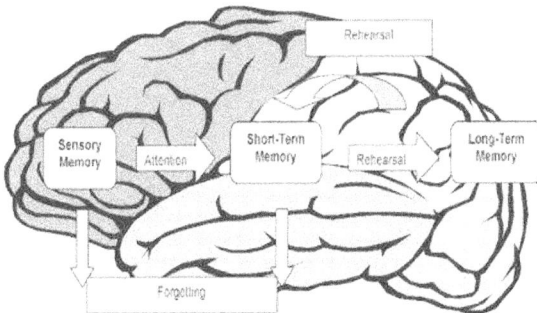

3. Perception

One of my favourite quotes by motivation guru Dr Wayne Dyer is, "When you change the way you look at things, the things you look at change." Your perception is the source of your point of view, your perspective. By exercising our ability to change our perception, we can shed limiting beliefs that block us or hold us back.

Perception is the act of form or conclusion about a subject or object, either via the information gained via the physical senses (sight, hearing, smell, taste and touch), or via the ideas we formulate regarding said subject or object.

Perception is relative, for example, when two people look at a glass that is filled half-way with water one person's perception is that the glass is half-full, while the other's is that it is half-empty.

This applies just as equally to the physical world, as to the non-physical world, the world of ideas. Evidence of this can clearly be seen all around. One person perceives opportunity, while simultaneously, another perceives lack or absence of opportunity. One perceives safety and security, while simultaneously, another perceives danger and uncertainty and soon.

4. Intuition

Are you intuitive? Intuition is what many call your sixth sense. It is what you refer to when you say, "Something doesn't feel right." It is a spiritual prompting, or personal revelation.

It is easy for us to dismiss our 'gut-feeling', or even worse, to dismiss our children's, when the truth is we are more powerful when we are in tune with our intuition and can use it to predict outcomes and make wise choices.

By consistently analysing your performance, you can quickly fine-tune your intuition, and become quite skilled at predicting various outcomes. Dr Wayne Dyer speaks of intuition as, "Guidance or as God talking, and this inner insight is never taken lightly or ignored."

We go to school and we go to work and we use our rational mind. We perform repetitive tasks and follow provided protocols. We conform to what society expects of us... we lather, rinse and repeat. We become faithful servants of a system we didn't create. Albert Einstein said it beautifully:

"The intuitive mind is a sacred gift, and the rational mind is a faithful servant. We have created a society that honours the servant and has forgotten the gift."

I guess that, like Einstein, I'm a fan of the illogic, the irrational, the seemingly impossible.

5. Will

The mental faculty called will gives us the ability to focus on a single idea and exclude everything else. This is a requirement for success because in order to create success, one must filter out negative thoughts, distractions, and people who may interfere with our success. This mental strength can be developed through practice, because what we focus on expands. Where there's a will, there's a way, they say. Or is it a"when?"

When I quit my job, there were times of obstacles, uncertainty, struggle, and doubt, but I focused on what could be, on the vision I was pursuing. Many years later, I don't regret a thing – even if some people don't understand or approve of my choice.

The proper use of the will is to keep a particular mental image fixed in the mind. It's pretty simple. No strain or great effort (what the ordinary layman might describe as willpower) is needed. To exercise force or creative agency, which is unnatural, is exhausting and once you exhaust your energy, the results obtained will inevitably dissipate also, says Dr Dyer.

6. Imagination
Imagination is the most marvellous and inconceivably powerful force that the world has ever known. The average person sadly uses this powerful tool against themselves. They imagine what they don't want, they imagine problems.

Let's begin to use our imagination the way God wanted us to use it. It is the greatest faculty that we possess and we can build anything we want with it. Just take a look and think about all the conveniences you have all around you. Some of these conveniences were not there 2, 5, 10 and 25 years ago. Do you know that every one of them without any exception was first created in the mind of one individual through imagination? Do you know that you can use your imagination to go into the future and bring it into the present? That's what highly successful people do.

They see where they want to go and they act like a person they want to become, they use the actor's technique, they use their imagination. Imagination may be simply defined as the formation of mental images or pictures. It is generally accepted that whenever people form a thought in their mind, they form an image which corresponds or matches the particular thought. For example, when you think of a dog, you form an image of a dog in your mind.

Thomas Edison had "Imagination is more powerful than knowledge" carved on his desk. Imagination is a miracle tool that allows us to find wonder in the mundane and to become a vessel for creative ideas to flow.

When we imagine a thing, place, or situation with emotional intensity, we produce the same emotional and biochemical reactions in our body as the actual experience. Humans are creative because we are children of a Creator; we're wonderfully and fearfully made in His image.

Are you using your six mental faculties to create freedom? By being conscious and aware of the tools you have at your disposal and using them properly, you can improve your quality of life.

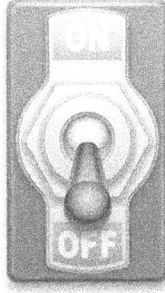

Flip that switch

Action Steps

➢ **Step 1**

Work smarter, not harder: What are some things you can do to exercise and develop your higher mental faculties and to encourage your kids to do the same?

Successful people have been studied exhaustively and have been found to be practicing these habits on a daily routine. Adding these to your daily routine will surely contribute greatly to your success.

1. Planning your day the day before. Plan what you want to accomplish before you even start your day. You do this before you retire in the evening. When you plan your day the night before, your subconscious mind then goes to work on your plans and goals while you are asleep. Preparing your daily list the night before will clear your mind and enable you to sleep more soundly which will increase your productivity throughout the day.

3. Make sure you're working from the 80/20 rule. If you have 10 items to do on your to do list, 2 of them will be more important than the other 8 put together. You can do this by asking yourself this question: if I were to go out of town by the close of business tomorrow, which 2 tasks of the 10 I would rather focus on? By knowing how to prioritise tasks and working from the list will increase your productivity by 25 - 50% each day.

4. Create time blocks dedicated to each task. Keep in mind that new tasks and responsibilities will come up continually, phone calls will come in, emails will come in and meetings will need to happen. The key to working smarter is also setting aside chunks of time for those unexpected tasks that will come up. Scheduling your time this way reduces stress and makes you feel in charge of your life.

5. Block time for breaks. Taking small breaks during the day will clear the air and give you some fresh starts to sharpen your focus. However, don't get too comfortable taking too many breaks thereby welcoming distractions. Most people spend about 50% of their time doing non-work related activities while they are at work. Break the time-wasting habits such as browsing social media, checking emails, taking long lunch breaks and chatting with co-workers. Time is your scarcest resource, you must work smarter to preserve it in any way possible and eliminating these time-wasting habits will improve your time management skills and your quality of life.

6. Spend your time like money. Even when you are not at work, your time is at least equal to your hourly rate. If a person or activity is asking you to donate your time, ask yourself how important is this task to me? And how much of my time and money am I willing to donate to it? If it's not important enough, you must discipline yourself not to do it, just say no! You want to give anytime to your priorities and your top 20% of your tasks first. Say no to tasks that don't move you forward or are not of high value. Ultimately your top goal everyday should be to get the highest return on your investment of your mental, physical and emotional energy, that's the key to working smarter.

➢ **Step 2**

Boost your creativity: Creativity has nothing to do with any activity in particular, it applies to everyone like artists, actors, musicians, etc. This simply means that anyone can be creative.

Creativity is action through inaction, you don't do creativity, it's not something you can do or produce, it's something that you can allow to happen. It's when you're in this state of inaction or the state of total relaxation that you can allow something to happen through.

To allow creativity, you need to achieve a state of total relaxation which is obviously easier said than done.

The reason I am saying it's easier said than done is because we are addicted to constant activities, either physical or mental, we always have this need to do. We are addicted to doing. How many times a day do you think you check your cell phone? You need to disconnect and relax and be with yourself. Action in inaction (relaxation) is something that just happens, it's immediate. It happens in places like a shower or going for a walk. The mind quietens down, you relax and that's when you have breakthroughs.

➢ **Step 3**

Improve your thinking ability: Instead of just making default decisions, you will be able to make thoughtful decisions and live your life by design.

1. Be Curious. When asked about an important trait they have, both Bill Gates and Warren Buffet had the same answer: curiosity. Curiosity pushes them to keep exploring the world and updating their model of the world. The model then helps them make the right decisions that lead them to success.

   I was curious about being self-employed when I was still employed. This led me to start my own business. Later, I became curious about motivational and professional speaking as well as writing books. This led me to become a motivational and professional speaker and writing this book. I often don't know where my curiosity would lead me. I just follow it because it's fun! But more often than not, it takes my life to the next level. Curiosity is a trait and so, it can be developed: explore the world around you; avoid labelling something as boring; become involved in side projects.

2. Read Diversely. I am always saddened when I hear some people saying they hate reading long text, they prefer short articles because they don't have time and long attention span. These people prefer being shallow as opposed to being deep. Remember insight lies in the details and not merely in the summary.

The quality of your output depends on the quality of your input. So, if you want to come up with good ideas, you need to feed your mind with good ideas. One way to do that is to read diversely for getting insights not for the mere sake of reading diverse topics. Learn to be diverse and yet deep. Why do you need to do this? Because it allows you to cross-pollinate the ideas in your mind. This will give you fresh new ideas. Don't just read from the fields you are familiar with; read from other fields as well.

3. Read actively. My favourite way to do this is by highlighting the book I read and reviewing them after I finish the book. I then put the actionable ideas in my idea journal. This helps me get the most out of the book. I also read the book more than once for maximum understanding. Once all this is done, I then put my ideas into action. Ideas without implementation remain ideas which are meaningless until they are put into practice.

4. Set time for mind exercise. Just as you should allocate time for physical exercise, you should also allocate time for mind exercise. This way you will improve your mind fitness the way people improve their physical fitness through exercise. Build picture puzzles and cross word puzzles, and play games like chess, Suduko, Monopoly and Pictionary.

5. Make a master list of problems. Make a list of problems you would like to solve. Since this is a live problem list, you should add new problems to it as you encounter them in your daily life without waiting for the exercise time to come. At the beginning of your mind exercise session, choose a problem from the master list which you need to solve. You will be more motivated to practice if you know that you need the solutions. The more you need the solution, the more motivated you will be. As you engage in this process of exercising your mind, you will generate ideas. To make sure that you do not lose the ideas you get through the exercise, write them down in an idea journal. Having an idea journal is useful.

➤ **Step 4**
Improve your memory: It was once believed that brain function peaked during early adulthood and then slowly declined, leading to lapses in memory and brain fog during your golden years. Now it's known that our modern lifestyle plays a significant role in contributing to cognitive decline, which is why exposure to toxins, chemicals, poor diet, lack of sleep and excessive stress, among others, hinder the functioning of your brain.

The flipside is also true; a healthy lifestyle can support your brain health and even encourage your brain to grow new neurons, a process known as neurogenesis. Dr Joseph Mercola, a world-renowned physician and New York Times bestselling author explains these things in his website, Mercola.com.

Your brain's hippocampus, that is the memory centre, is able to grow new cells and it's now known that your hippocampus regenerates throughout your entire lifetime (even into your 90s), provided you give it the tools to do so. These "tools" are primarily lifestyle-based, which is wonderful news. You don't need an expensive prescription medication or any medical procedure at all to boost your brain, and your memory. You can simply apply the following tips by Dr Mercola:

1. Eat right. The foods you eat – and don't eat – play a crucial role in your memory. Fresh vegetables are essential, as are healthy fats and avoiding sugar and grain carbohydrates.

    Curry, celery, broccoli, cauliflower, and walnuts contain antioxidants and other compounds that protect your brain health and may even stimulate the production of new brain cells.

    Increasing your animal-based omega-3 fat intake and reducing consumption of damaged omega-6 fats (think processed vegetable oils) in order to balance your omega-3 to omega-6 ratio, is also important.

    I prefer krill oil to fish oil, as krill oil also contains astaxanthin, which not only protects the omega-3 fats from oxidation but also appears to be particularly beneficial for brain health.

Coconut oil is another healthful fat for brain function. According to research by Dr Mary Newport just over two tablespoons of coconut oil (about 35 ml or 7 level teaspoons) would supply you with the equivalent of 20 grams of medium-chain triglycerides (MCT), which is indicated as either a preventative measure against degenerative neurological diseases, or as a treatment for an already established case.

2. Exercise. Anything that's good for your heart is good for your head. Exercise encourages your brain to work at optimum capacity by stimulating nerve cells to multiply, strengthening their interconnections and protecting them from damage. During exercise nerve cells release proteins known as neurotrophic factors. One in particular, called brain-derived neurotrophic factor (BDNF), triggers numerous other chemicals that promote neural health, and directly benefits cognitive functions, including learning.

Doctors are reporting an increase in number of people with Alzheimer's and dementia (memory loss and thinking) because technology is doing everything for you.
We are not realising we are losing our minds. We are really forgetting how to do things by ourselves. Remember, what you practice in private, you are rewarded for in public.
A 2010 study on primates published in Neuroscience also revealed that regular exercise not only improved blood flow to the brain, but also helped the monkeys learn new tasks twice as quickly as non-exercising monkeys.

This is a benefit the researchers believe would hold true for people as well. In a separate one year-long study, individuals who engaged in exercise were actually growing and expanding the brain's memory centre one to two percent per year, where typically that centre would have continued to decline in size. To get the most out of your workouts, I recommend a comprehensive program that includes high-intensity interval exercise, strength training, stretching, and core work, along with regular intermittent movement.

3. Stop multitasking. Used for decades to describe the parallel processing abilities of computers, multitasking is now shorthand for the human attempt to do simultaneously as many things as possible, as quickly as possible.

   Ultimately, multitasking may actually slow you down, make you prone to errors as well as make you forgetful.
   Research shows you actually need about eight seconds to commit a piece of information to your memory, so if you're talking on your phone and carrying in groceries when you put down your car keys, you're unlikely to remember where you left them.

   The opposite of multitasking would be mindfulness, which helps you achieve undistracted focus. Students who took a mindfulness class improved reading comprehension test scores and working memory capacity, as well as experienced fewer distracting thoughts.

If you find yourself trying to complete five tasks at once, stop yourself and focus your attention back to the task at hand. If distracting thoughts enter your head, remind yourself that these are only "projections," not reality, and allow them to pass by without stressing you out.

4. Get enough sleep. Research from Harvard indicates that people are 33% more likely to infer connections among distantly related ideas after sleeping, but few realise that their performance has actually improved. Sleep is also known to enhance your memories and help you "practice" and improve your performance of challenging skills. In fact, a single night of sleeping only four to six hours can impact your ability to think clearly the next day.
   The process of brain growth, or neuroplasticity, is believed to underlie your brain's capacity to control behaviour, including learning and memory. Plasticity occurs when neurons are stimulated by events, or information, from the environment. However, sleep and sleep loss modify the expression of several genes and gene products that may be important for synaptic plasticity.

Furthermore, certain forms of long-term potentiation, a neural process associated with the laying down of learning and memory, can be elicited in sleep, suggesting synaptic connections are strengthened while you slumber.

5. Play brain games. If you don't sufficiently challenge your brain with new, surprising information, it eventually begins to deteriorate. What research into brain plasticity shows us, however, is that by providing your brain with appropriate stimulus, you can counteract this degeneration. One way to challenge your brain is via 'brain games,' which you can play online via Web sites like Lumosity.com.

   If you decide to try brain games, ideally it would be wise to invest at least 20 minutes a day, but no more than five to seven minutes is to be spent on a specific task. When you spend longer amounts of time on a task, the benefits weaken. If you don't enjoy brain games, you can also try learning a new skill or hobby.

6. Master a new skill. A key factor necessary for improving your brain function or reversing functional decline is the seriousness of purpose with which you engage in a task. In other words, the task must be important to you, or somehow meaningful or interesting — it must hold your attention.

   For instance, one study revealed that craft activities such as quilting and knitting were associated with decreased odds of having mild cognitive impairment. Another study, published earlier this year, found that taking part in "cognitively demanding" activities like learning to quilt or take digital photography enhanced memory function in older adults. The key is to find an activity that is mentally stimulating for you. Ideally this should be something that requires your undivided attention and gives you great satisfaction... it should be an activity that you look forward to doing, such as playing a musical instrument, gardening, building model ships and crafting, to mention a few.

7. Try mnemonic devices. Mnemonic devices are memory tools to help you remember words, information or concepts. They help you to organise information into an easier-to-remember format. Try:
   o Acronyms (such as PUG for "pick up grapes")
   o Visualisations (such as imagining a tooth to remember your dentist's appointment)

   o Rhymes (if you need to remember a name, for instance, think "Shirley's hair is curly)
   o Chunking, which is breaking up information into smaller "chunks" (such as organising numbers into the format of a phone number)

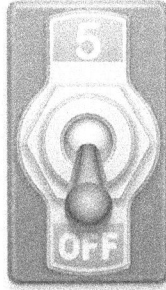

The best story ever told

"When I was a child, I talked like a child, I reasoned like a child. When I became a man, I put the ways of childhood behind me."
– St Paul, (AD 5 – AD 67), apostle of Jesus Christ as quoted in the Holy Bible, 1 Corinthians 13:11

I'm sure that at some stage someone came up to you and asked casually," So, what's your story?" In a split second you had to decide whether to smile sweetly and say nothing, or to tell your story.

Each of us has a personal story, a history of things that have happened to us. Our personal stories shape us. And truth be told, we tend to live our lives according to what happened in the past and not according to what we can make happen in the future.

Our personal stories are true and are, very often, sad. I must emphasise, though, that there are always different interpretations of the same story. It is the interpretation of the story that ultimately determines how the story affects and shapes your entire life.

The story cannot be changed, because whatever happened, happened. The interpretation, however, can be changed. I can hear you silently asking, "But how do I change the interpretation of my true sad story?"

Here is my own story: My father was brutally stabbed and murdered when I was seven years old. When I was sixteen years old, my beloved mother was tragically knocked down by a car, whose driver had been shot dead in a botched hijacking and lost control of the car.

The car went straight into my mother, so fast that she couldn't avoid it, knocked her down and dragged her along the side of the road going over electrical boxes, poles and fences. She died instantly. Her body parts were scattered all over the place and were picked up one by one and put inside a body bag.

As if that wasn't enough, hardly two years later, my eldest brother, who was taking care of me and had grown close to me, also died. I had just passed my first year tertiary examinations and as part of celebrating that achievement, he had planned a few fun activities.

For starters, we were going to watch a soccer match at Soccer City, the final between Kaizer Chiefs and Witbank Black Aces. When that fateful Saturday arrived, my gut wouldn't allow me to go. I felt so unwell that I ended up deciding not to go to the match. However, I accompanied my brother to a taxi and I personally opened the door for him to enter. That was the last time I saw him alive. He never came back.

It took two painful years for us as a family to eventually discover that he had died. He died under mysterious circumstances and was buried as a pauper or unknown person with no family – despite all our efforts to find him. This painful experience also took a toll on me.

There were other painful incidents that happened after those, but God the Almighty gave me strength and wisdom to change the interpretation of my story.

I shared my sad story with my mentor Les Brown in 2013 when I first met him. He sympathised with me and shared his sad story with me. "Veli, I and my twin brother Wesley were born on the floor of an old building. We were adopted. I am 69 years old now. If a man and a woman were to show up now and say they were my biological parents, I wouldn't know if they were telling the truth. I never saw them, not even a picture of them. But   I refused to be defined by my story." Today, Les Brown is one of the top motivational speakers in the world and has made millions of dollars. You can find out more about him on his official website www.lesbrown.com.

Anyway, that night, after my conversation with Les, I couldn't sleep a wink. It dawned on me that I was using my sad personal story as an excuse to justify why I wasn't following my dream. Yes, I couldn't change what had happened to me in the past, but I could determine my future.

I realised how lucky I was to be alive and, secondly, how lucky I was to know who my parents were. It dawned on me that it could have been worse. I had fond memories of my parents, unlike Les Brown, the icon of motivational speaking. I then vowed that I would never use my story as an excuse. Instead, I'd use it to empower myself and others.

I am not sharing this story with you to seek pity, for you to feel sorry for me or to impress you. I am sharing my story to express to you that there's always a way out of your situation. You see, most people are held back by their personal stories and are always seeking pity and comfort from the world. Wake up and use your story to propel you to the top.

Don't let your story sabotage your dreams, however sad it may be. Look at it this way: it could have been worse; you could have died and missed the opportunity to live. Be grateful that you are alive and have the world as a platform to step up and express your gifts and talents.

There's a story of a man who lived with his wife and twin sons. I heard the story, but I don't know if it's true or if it's an urban legend. Whichever way, it's still a useful story to demonstrate the power of personal stories. So, this man was an alcoholic. He was abusive to his family, especially to his wife.

He would go and get drunk with his friends and when he came back home, he would kick things around, swear at his family and even beat them up for no reason. The family lived like this for many years. When the twin boys turned 19 years of age, they left home and went to live in two different cities far from each other. They started their own lives and families in these two cities.

One boy grew up to be a fine man, a good husband to his wife and a fantastic father to his children. His community looked up to him as role model.

The other twin boy became a scruffy alcoholic exactly like his father. He became abusive to his family and was troublesome even to his community. His life was used as an example of how not to live. He was an embarrassment to everyone.

When these two men were asked individually as to why their lives turned out to be the way they were, they gave the same answer. The answer was, "What else could you expect with a father like mine?" The bad man used his father's bad behaviour to justify his own bad behaviour. The good man, however, said, "I made a decision that I would never be like my father. Though the same thing happened to both men – they shared the same story – their interpretation of their story and their responses to their story were completely different. This once again, shows that we cannot change what happens to us, but we can adjust how we interpret it. We can either take it personally (which leads to bitterness, anger and holding grudges) or decide to interpret it differently.

In my case, I asked myself later on as to what could have happened if I had been the one who died instead of my loved ones? The answer to this question forced me to change my perspective. I started to realise how fortunate I was to be alive. I learned to appreciate life even more. Living a life of appreciation made me want to help other people appreciate their lives irrespective of what happened to them in the past.

The second verse of the Serenity Prayer written by American theologian Reinhold Niebuhr says, "Living one day at a time; Enjoying one moment at a time; Accepting hardships as the pathway to peace; Taking, as He did, this sinful world As it is, not as I would have it; Trusting that he will make all things right if I surrender to His Will; So that I may be reasonably happy in this life And supremely happy with Him Forever and ever in the next. Amen."

These words are about acceptance. There cannot be serenity without first reaching acceptance. What we resist persists. Acceptance doesn't resist, wrestle, regret, deny, or excuse. It merely accepts what is just as it is without trying to change it. Acceptance can also mean that we trust God with the matter.

This is the same as forgiving. Forgiveness is not only an act of freeing others from what they have done to you. It is also an act of wisdom that frees you from what was done to you. The circumstance or situation itself can't be changed, but the meaning of it can be.
I can safely say that you have the power to change yourself and you need courage to do so. You don't have the power to change people, places, or things and serenely accepting this fact is a blessing.

Don't be a prisoner of your story. Whatever happened, happened. However painful, accept that it did happen. Seek a different meaning as I have done with my life story. Read and listen to other people's stories and you will realise that yours is really not the worst personal narrative.

Change comes when you accept what is and search for a different meaning. And wisdom comes when you accept something as it is, not as you want it to be. When you allow this to happen in your life, change will take place because change is a sign of wisdom and serenity.

The world is a better place today than what it was many years ago, not because wise men and women changed it but because they changed the way they looked at it.

Our ancestors didn't change the rain and the heat from the sun. No. They invented an umbrella and a rain coat, instead. They didn't prevent the night and darkness from falling, but they discovered fire and invented the light bulb.

All the pains, disappointments, setbacks and failures I went through were worthwhile because they introduced me to the Veli Ndaba I did not know existed. As I am writing these words right now, I am communicating to that part of you that senses your life can be better.

This part of you believes in your greatness, but you have drowned it through procrastination and fear. Throughout the years, you have probably justified your inaction, citing your sad personal story as a reason.

What if you do something different this time? Take your sad story and store it as the first chapter of your life. Then start writing the second and third happier chapters of your life. Give it a Cinderella twist, if you'd like. Just give it a try. Re-write your script. It may yet become the best story ever told.

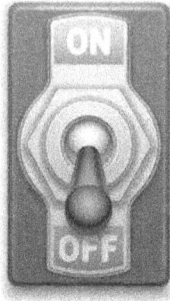

Flip that switch
Action Steps

➤ **Step 1**

Write down your personal story (a summary only)

➤ **Step 2**

What would you like the next chapter of your life story to be? Write down.

➤ **Step 3**

What can you do right now to start your new chapter? Write down some ideas. Feel free to pray and ask for Divine favour and guidance at this point.

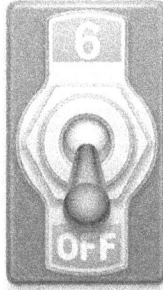

Attracting the good stuff

"Running after a butterfly only chases it away and wastes your precious time. By making yourself bright and colourful, you attract the butterfly to you."
– Veli Ndaba, South African author and motivational speaker

Weeds don't need any encouragement to grow. You don't have to water them. You don't have to give them fertilizer. They grow anywhere, anytime, even through the cracks of a side walk. But if you want to grow orchids or roses or any kind of exotic flower, there are special processes and procedures you must go through. By the same token, you don't have to force yourself or motivate yourself to think negatively, to be depressed, to hate somebody, to beat yourself up over your head or feel loaded with guilt. When your mind is on automatic, it will do that by itself. It can come up with the most horrendous thoughts. You can be perfectly peaceful the one moment and worried sick the next moment with the thought, 'what if I die tomorrow?' Your mind excels at playing nasty tricks like that.

Therefore, if you want to move into your own personal greatness, if you want to enjoy a joyful, successful and healthy life, you've got to take control of your mind. You have to water and fertilise good thoughts and pull out the

bad thoughts or weeds of your mind, to use the analogy of plants. You've got to harness your will and say, "I am in control here."

You see, the body has limitations but the mind doesn't. We tend to focus on what happens from the neck down, yet the truth is that it all starts in the mind. If you are not mentally ready, you will never be physically prepared for anything. All the preparation begins in the mind.

I truly believe that all of us on this planet have gifts and your task every day is to figure out what yours is. You'll really never find peace in your life until you figure it out. Once you figure out what it is, you then need to decide whether to act on it or not. Who do you look up to? What excites you when you wake up in the morning? What legacy do you want to leave behind? What do you want to be known for? What thoughts do you want to have? Only you can decide.

You often hear people say that if you want to know who holds you back from greatness, just look in the mirror. In my opinion, it's not who you see in the mirror that holds you back; what you see in the mirror is merely your physical reflection. The one that really holds you back is the one you don't see, your mind. Do you agree?

Until you find your gifts, keep on searching, keep on investing in yourself in the form of books, workshops, coaching, mentorship and other forms of personal development interventions because you are your own biggest asset.

Complaining about everything around you won't help you in anyway. You can never solve a level five problem with a level two solution. In any situation in your life, you are the solution. It's always about whether you are bigger or smaller than the problem you are faced with. You have a huge capacity to grow as a solution. Grappling with the same problem over and over again is an indication that you are not growing as a solution.

The issue is not what is happening to you; the issue is your response to what is happening to you. So, grow your mind, it's the only solution and determinant of how your life turns out. The better you grow it, the quicker you can deal with your challenges. Hoping that it just thrives by itself is a recipe for heartache and frustration.

The main reason most people are stuck in 'Loserville' is what I call comparison paradigm. There are basically two paradigms, namely 1) the self-acceptance paradigm and 2) the comparison paradigm. Self- acceptance paradigm is about running your own race; it's about being true to yourself. It's about working on improving your own time every time you run rather than pushing against all odds to become first. There's peace of mind in the self-acceptance paradigm.

Comparison paradigm is about comparing yourself with others and wanting to be better than them. If you make R100 000 a year, the truth is there are people who are making ten times more than that amount in the same period. In all aspects, there'll be someone better than you. So, you can never win in this paradigm. This means that unless you fix the inner issue and your perspective about life, you will never have peace and stability in your life.

When your happiness is dependent on outside forces, you will never be at peace with yourself. It's very important to sit down and have an honest conversation with yourself about the type of life you want to lead and what things will personally fulfil you. It is crucial to remember that everyone's notion of success is and will always be subjective. Also remember that there's never enough time to do everything, but there's always enough time to do the most important things. Taking control of your mind, weeding out bad thoughts and replacing them with good ones are very important things – start doing it right now and you will see how good things and good people start arriving in your life.

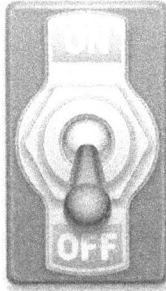

Flip that switch
Action Steps

> ➤ **Step 1**
Answer the questions below.
1. What excites you when you wake up in the morning? The following things get me excited

2. What legacy do you wish to leave behind? I wish to leave behind

3. What do you want to be known for? I want to be known for

4. Which bad thoughts do you need to weed out?
I need to weed out

> ➤ **Step 2**
Decide on the 'good stuff' you want to attract and affirm. Imagine there are no limits.
I am attracting

> **Step 3**

Develop a questioning mindset.

Albert Einstein said, "If I had an hour to solve a problem and my life was dependent on the solution, I would spend the first fifty-five minutes determining the proper question to ask, for once I know the proper question to ask, I could solve the problem in less than five minutes."

If asking good questions is so critical, why don't most of us spend more of our time and energy on discovering and framing them? One critical reason may be that our educational system focuses more on memorisation and right answers than on the art of seeking new possibilities. We are rarely asked to discover compelling questions, nor are we taught why we should ask such questions in the first place.

Quizzes, examinations, and aptitude tests all reinforce the value of correct answers. The avoidance in our culture to asking creative questions is linked to an emphasis on finding quick fixes. The reward systems in our organisations further reinforce this dilemma. Leaders believe that they are paid for fixing problems rather than for fostering breakthrough thinking. Between our attachment to black/white, either/or thinking and our anxiety about not knowing, we have thwarted our collective capacity for deep creativity and fresh perspectives.

A paradigm shift occurs when a question is asked inside the current paradigm that can only be answered from outside it. It is this kind of paradigm shift, based on powerful questions, that may be necessary to create truly innovative solutions to our most pressing concerns. An example of this is a popular nine dots IQ test question where you have to connect nine dots with four lines without lifting the pencil from the paper.

The main reason why most people fail to get this quiz correct is because they look for the answer inside the box. The minute you take the lines outside the box, the answer is found. So, to change the current paradigm, one must consider looking outside of it by asking powerful questions.

➤ **Step 4**
Challenge your current beliefs.
Why do I strongly believe what I believe? Is it because:
I tested it?
I was told about it? I personally saw it?
I personally experienced it? – 'Once bitten, twice shy.'

Habits

"The diminutive chains of habit are seldom felt until they are too strong to be broken."
– Samuel Johnson (1709 – 1789), English writer and father of the modern dictionary

There's not much new that I can tell you about habits, is there? We all have them. Some are good and some are bad. You know your habits well, your family and close friends probably know your habits too. And even your pets may know your habits, as those of us that have cats and dogs can testify.

Our dogs know more or less what time we are due to arrive from work every day and go stand by the gate or front door, wagging their tails in great anticipation.

It's very easy to get into the habit of doing something in a particular way and at a particular time, and so it follows that it's easy to form new habits. Getting rid of – or breaking a habit – is however, quite a difficult process for most us.

So what is a habit? I like Wikipedia's simple definition: a habit is a routine of behaviour that is repeated regularly and tends to occur subconsciously. There's a whole psychological process in the making and breaking of habits. In a nutshell, we have habits because we are creatures that like routine, comfort and safety. Habits – even the bad ones – give us that desired routine and comfort.

I suggest that you put your habits under the magnifying glass so that you can understand which habits are working to your advantage and which ones are holding you back. In chapter 2 of this book, we speak about knowing yourself and as habits are part and parcel of who you are, you better get to know them too. No, don't go into denial about habits. You know what they say, it's healthier to swim the Nile (Africa's longest river) than to go into denial regarding a problem.

Jokes aside, habits can make you or block you, so let's take a quick look at the basic facts. Habits are formed gradually – not at a stroke. Great change may come over your character without you even being conscious of it. This is the power of habit. You need energy and discipline to unlock the power of habit in your life.

You often hear people saying "I wonder where he/she gets so much energy". But we don't actually get or gain energy...we release it. Science has proven this. How does one access this energy? Through desire. Desire is the triggering mechanism that lets the energy flow through you. The amount of desire you have determines the amount of energy you will release.

Having discipline means doing something you hate in order to create something you love. So, in order to build habits in your life, you need to apply discipline. Science has proven that it takes, on average, 66 days to form a habit. Just build one at a time. Focus on building one habit now and get it done and then move on to the next one. Over time these habits will rule your life.

Don't get so distracted by the glory of success that you miss the source of success: the boring, fundamental and foundational little things done over and over, and over again.

There's a certain natural progression in life: you plant, cultivate and then harvest. We seem to have been conditioned to try jump straight from planting to harvest, but you can't skip the middle part, the cultivation, and hope to master the mundane little things overnight. It just doesn't work that way. You have to understand the power and the secret of time and learn to be patient (which means applying discipline).

We are conditioned, for an example, to watch a two-hour action packed movie, forgetting that the movie is the result of three years of work (sometimes more) condensed down into two hours. It is important to remember that the story and the characters captured on film don't only take two hours to unfold in real life. The progression of a character going from a nobody to winning a boxing championship doesn't happen within two hours in real life.

You have to tolerate the mundane and be willing to put in the hours of practicing your craft over and over again in order to get ahead in life.

The real world is often portrayed in artificial snapshots by many who are addicted to climactic (climax) moments (only chasing results). Reality is not boring. You just need to remember that you are not living in a two- hour movie.

Understand that the routine that leads to greatness and success is not flashy, it's not at all glorious, heroic, exciting and dramatic. It is boring and mundane. It's about doing little simple things every single day.

The paradox about doing simple, easy things is that they are simple to do but not necessarily easy to do. An example of this paradox is getting on top of your diet. Everyone knows how to be healthy and get in shape. It's not magic and also not difficult. But most people still don't do it.

You know what to eat, but you are just not doing it – and not because it's difficult. The formula is to stop eating unhealthy burgers and eat the greens instead. This is straightforward and doesn't require any specific skill
besides simple discipline. This is so easy to do! Do this for about three years or so and you'll be healthy. Don't expect it to happen in two hours though. Remember that a two-hour action-packed movie represents three years plus of work condensed down into two hours.

Whenever one succeeds at something, that one glorious and exciting moment is a representation of a lot of sacrifices, sweat, tears and tiny little actions compounded over time. It's not just about making a wish and waving a magic wand that produces results, no. It's taking little – mostly boring – steps repeatedly over a long period of time.

When you board an airplane you have a choice of whether you'll listen to some music or to an audio book, whether you are going to watch a movie or read a book, it's easy to do and it's easy not to do.

Where do you think you would be today if you were reading 10 pages of an inspirational book every day for the past three years? You would definitely be a different person now, in a completely different situation. You won't have to do anything glorious. Just read 10 pages every single day, that's it.

Always remember the three steps of the process of life: 1) planting, 2) cultivating and 3) harvesting. Carrying a seed in your hand, however expensive it may be, will not guarantee you a harvest. For your seed to be of value, you need to plant it. The minute you plant it, weeds show up. And if you don't eradicate the weeds and cultivate your plant, it will die. The seed represents ideas, thoughts, intentions and good wishes. These don't mean anything until they are implemented.

Implementation alone doesn't guarantee success, though. Negativity, doubt, naysayers and laziness will creep in and have to be uprooted for you to stay the course, to keep growing. Otherwise, all the good ideas, intentions and wishes will shrivel and die by harvest time.

Success (or harvest) is mainly determined by your attitude towards cultivation or how you deal with weeds. If you don't eradicate it, it will take over your garden and kill everything you've planted.

This represent people who give up to challenges and hardships (weeds) that they encounter along the way and they give up. We can all learn so much from this analogy. Almost every successful person begins with two beliefs in mind:

1. The future can be better than the present.
2. I have the power to make it happen.

Excellence is the gradual result of being in the habit of always striving to do better. It doesn't happen in one day – it happens every day. This excellence is not a skill, but an attitude. It's this attitude that leads you to success. This simply tells you that the extent of your impact on this world depends on the size of your devotion to this attitude.

Aristotle said it so well: "We are what we repeatedly do. Excellence, therefore is not an act, but a habit." Living a good life is about doing ordinary things extraordinarily well. Day in, day out. Year in and year out.

Do you believe that the future can be better than the present for you? Remember, life doesn't give us what we want, but what we are. What we are, is what we believe is true for us. You attract what you believe. So, I can safely say that your belief system is like a magnet that attracts situations and people that are like-minded or with similar beliefs. This is how the world conspires with you.

If you really want to change the results you are producing, you need to align your belief system and your habits with what you want. There's no way you'll have a better future if you don't believe in it. Whenever you apportion blame and complain, you give away your God-given power to handle the situation at hand.

Study successful people that you admire and you'll realise that they were just like you, if not worse. But they believed that the future was going to be better. They believed they were worthy of success and then took action to make success happen.

You need to believe that you have the power to make it happen. You are a one-time miracle that was brought down here on earth by God to fulfil a particular purpose. Your parents were not issued with a manual when you were born, but your heart carries your desires – and desires are an indication of what you are meant to do. Don't allow external voices and opinions of people to drown your inner voice.

I was born to help you create the silence in your heart that will help you listen to that voice of reason, which you have allowed to be drowned by people who don't even know themselves. My purpose in life is to inspire and empower you to realise your true potential and live your dreams.

I believe you can break bad habits and acquire new habits. I believe that:

> 1. Your future can be much better than the "present."
> 2. You have the power to make it happen.

So, go ahead, break the chains and make it "happen."

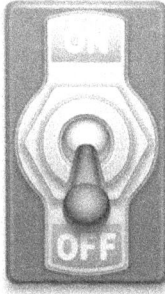

Flip that switch

Action Steps

> **Step 1**

Write down your 5 best habits

> **Step 2**

Write down your 5 worst habits

> **Step 3**

Write down the habits that you want to change in the next few months

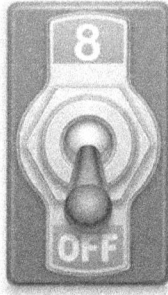

Changing Habits

"The need for change bulldozed a road down the centre of my mind."
– Maya Angelou (1928 – 2014), American poet, singer, memoirist, and civil rights activist

James Clear, who shares science-based ideas for living a better life and building habits that stick, wrote an excellent article in the Huffington Post in 2014 (https://www.huffingtonpost.com/james-clear/forming-new-habits_b_5104807.html). The article is titled, How Long Does It Actually Take to Form a New Habit? (Backed by Science) and it reads:

Dr Maxwell Maltz was a plastic surgeon in the 1950s when he began noticing a strange pattern among his patients. Whenever he performed an operation – like a nose job, for example – he found that it would take the patients about 21 days to get used to seeing their new face.
Similarly, when a patient had an arm or a leg amputated, Dr Maltz noticed that the patient would sense a phantom limb for about 21 days before adjusting to the new situation.

He noted down these experiences and said, "These, and many other commonly observed phenomena tend to show that it requires a minimum of about 21 days for an old mental image to dissolve and a new one jell."

In 1960, Maltz published that quote and his other thoughts on behaviour change in a book called Psycho-Cybernetics. The book went on to become a blockbuster, selling more than 30 million copies worldwide. But a few decades later, Phillipa Lally, a health psychology researcher at University College London, and her research team decided to figure out just how long it actually takes to form a habit.

The study examined the habits of 96 people over a 12-week period. Each person chose one new habit for the 12 weeks and reported each day on whether or not they did the behaviour and how automatic the behaviour felt.

Some people chose simple habits like "drinking a bottle of water with lunch." Others chose more difficult tasks like "running for 15 minutes before dinner." At the end of 12 weeks, the researchers analysed the data to determine how long it took each person to go from starting a new behaviour to automatically doing it.

The answer? On average, it takes more than two months before a new behaviour becomes automatic – 66 days to be exact. And how long it takes a new habit to form can vary widely depending on the behaviour, the person, and the circumstances. In Lally's study, it took anywhere from 18 days to 254 days for people to form a new habit. The study results were published in the European Journal of Social Psychology on 16 July 2009.

Now you know how the average of 66 days to form a new habit was scientifically arrived at. Just use your discipline to build one habit at a time, focus on one now and get it done and move on to the next one and over time these good and well- planned habits will rule your life.

Our habits are the things that drive our results. The reality is that people make habits and then habits make people. It's sad that most people haven't yet come to this realisation.

Armed with this powerful information on habit formation, I went on to study successful people. What I found was that successful people have the same amount of time and days as I have, as well as the same amount of self-discipline. The only difference is that they deliberately form good habits and allow good habits to drive their lives.

This discovery led me to identify a few habits that I needed to get into. These habits were going to help me produce better results than I was producing at the time.
I started to wake up in the morning and drink two glasses of water to rehydrate my body. I started to create a gratitude list of about five to 10 things every morning; things like my wonderful family, my well-functioning brain, the opportunities that God has made possible for me and the clean air that I breathe. Science has proven that by focusing on the positive things in your life, your happiness level increase by up to 25%, which is a fantastic thing for the morning.

I stopped watching and listening to the news and reading newspapers in the morning to protect myself from negativity and distractions.

I changed my training times from the evenings to the mornings. Exercise like playing squash for me does wonders for my body, brain and overall well-being. I started to collect audio books and motivational CDs for when I am driving around. These help reinforce a positive mind-set. How you start your day sets the tone for your day. When you get to the office you are oozing with energy and positivity.

I also started to watch what I was eating, starting off with a healthy breakfast. These are the habits that I installed and now they are driving me; making it possible for me to produce more and better results than before. Health, wealth, love and happiness are the main areas I focus my life on when I identify the results I want to produce. In my experience, after about two months of focusing on a new habit, you don't have to think about it anymore; it takes over and you do it automatically.

The question is how do we deliberately create habits? It's important to know that the brain likes to put things on autopilot, which is an automatic mode. But you want to always be conscious of and in control of your habits, be they motor habits, intellectual or emotional habits.

Motor habits refer to muscular activities of an individual. These are habits related to our physical actions, such as: standing, sitting, running, walking, doing, exercise and maintaining particular postures of body. Intellectual habits are related to psychological processes requiring our intellectual abilities such as good observation, accurate perception, logical thinking, using of reasoning ability before taking decisions and testing conclusions.

Emotional habits include helping others who are in need, trusting people, being honest, and talking in a friendly way. The subject of habits has been studied exhaustively and in The Power of Habit, award-winning New York Times business reporter Charles Duhigg takes us to the thrilling edge of scientific discoveries that explain why habits exist and how they can be changed. With penetrating intelligence and an ability to distil vast amounts of information into engrossing narratives, Duhigg brings to life a whole new understanding of human nature and its potential for transformation.

At its core, The Power of Habit contains an exhilarating argument: the key to exercising regularly, losing weight, raising exceptional children, becoming more productive, building revolutionary companies and social movements, and achieving success is understanding how habits work.

To change your life, you firstly need to understand how habits work and what it takes to change them. The truth is, every habit functions the same way, it follows a habit loop. At first there's a Cue, some type of a trigger that makes the behaviour unfold automatically. Studies tell us that a cue can be a location, a time of day, a certain emotional state, other people or just a pattern of behaviours that consistently triggers a certain routine.

The next part in the habit loop is the Routine, the behaviour itself. The last part of the habit loop is the Reward, and in some respects the reward is the most important because that's why habits exist (so that we can get the rewards that we want). But figuring out a reward can be tricky. Duhigg did a bit of an experiment on himself to figure out what reward was driving his habit of eating a chocolate cookie in the afternoons between 3pm and 3:30pm.

One day when the cookie urge struck, instead of going out to the cafeteria, he went outside and took a walk around the block. The next day he went back to the cafeteria as usual, but instead of buying a cookie, he bought a candy bar and then ate it at his desk. And then the day after that, he again went back to the cafeteria. But he didn't buy anything. Instead, he talked to friends for about 10 minutes.

What he was trying to do, was to test different hypothesis to figure out what reward he was actually craving. What he figured out pretty quickly was that it had nothing to do with cookies, it had to do with socialising. What he eventually did, was that when that 'cookie' time came, he would stand up and look around the office, walk over to a friendly person and have a chat for few minutes, and then go back to his desk. The urge to go get a cookie completely disappeared and a new behaviour had become a habit – and he lost about 6kg as a result.

Studies have shown that if you can diagnose your habits, you can change them in whichever way you want. So, what are the cues, routines and rewards in your life? What habit do you want to change? Go ahead and do it now.

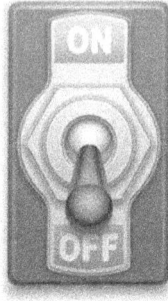

Flip that switch
Action Steps

➤ **Step 1**

Analyse the habits that you want to change and describe why and how you intend changing them.

Habit1:

Why I am going to change it:

The cue is:

The routine is:

The reward is:

The plan to change it:

The starting date for change:

Habit2:

Why I'm going to change it:

The cue is:

The routine is:

The reward is:

The plan to change it:

The starting date for change:

➤ **Step 2**

Implement your plan according to the starting date that you've chosen. All the best.

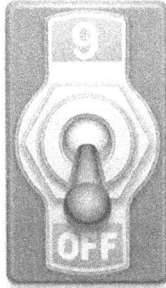

Effectiveness and efficiency

"You must attend to your business with the vendor in the market, and not to the noise of the market."
– Old African proverb, from Benin region

Effectiveness is about doing the right things while efficiency is about doing things right, according to management consultant Peter Ducker.

If you can manage to do the right things well (or right) most of the time, you are guaranteed to make your dreams come true. Doing the right things badly won't give you great results. And doing the wrong things in the most excellent way, won't help you either, because two wrongs never make one right!

In the past, I was always asking myself why some people were more successful than me. This led me to study successful people in the world and to learn about the fundamental differences between myself and them. One of these fundamental differences was the use of time.

I used to wake up in the morning and grab my mobile phone, check my WhatsApp, Facebook and LinkedIn messages before anything else. I would then proceed to check my emails, watch the news on TV and listen to the news while driving to work. But after studying successful people, especially those in the field I wanted to dedicate my entire life on, my approach to time changed altogether.

I discovered that successful people separate themselves from the noise of the world in order to have clarity of purpose. They treasure time. They don't waste time. And they don't allow others to waste their time. I learnt that our ability to control our time, especially the first and the last hours of the day, is very important. It's said that you win the first hour of the day to win the rest of the day.

Don't pick up your phone first thing in the morning to check your messages or social media. This is where most people give away their power and control. I say you give your power away, because you open yourself up to respond and react to the world's needs and demands first thing in the morning before you have even prepared yourself for the day ahead. This trains your brain to respond and react to things that are outside of your sphere of influence. Why use your precious time on unworthy 'news' that others dump on social media platforms? Don't train your brain to be dictated to; you will end up being distracted and side-tracked throughout the entire day as you have to respond, react, like, share and comment on trivialities.

My morning ritual for the first two hours of the day is to meditate, pray, drink two to three glasses of water to rehydrate my body, write down three personal and business things I want to focus on and get done by the end of the day.

This works for me. I don't get myself lost on a long list of hundreds of things to do, no, I just focus on a few. Don't allow your brain to be hacked and manipulated by other people's demands so early in the morning. There are many distractions and enemies out there that are literally rewiring and retraining your brain to be ineffective.

There's a term called Facebook depression (FD) which refers to the condition of spending too much time on social media sites such as Facebook. This is about constantly checking your social media feeds and comparing your life to the highlights of other people's lives. Going online and checking on the status of our various Facebook friends (many of whom we have never
met in real life) often forces us to deal with people who are either a) more successful than we are, or b) more attractive than we are. Whether or not this is actually the case, Facebook users may tend to regard themselves as "competing" with their various Facebook friends and can often feel inadequate as a result. Some individuals may be more prone to Facebook depression depending on:

- How many Facebook friends they have
- How much time they spend reading updates from a wide circle of friends
- How frequently they read updates
- How many of the updates are actually nothing more than bragging

Status updates in which friends announce significant achievements or display how successful they are (bragging), are more likely to attract attention.

Facebook users are also more likely to pay attention to profiles that are already popular (including ones that have a large number of Facebook friends, 'Likes' or which attract numerous comments). Other factors such as physical attractiveness may also make some profiles more popular than others, especially if the user is an attractive female.

Everybody seems to be competing about updating their status, showing new things they have acquired, materially or otherwise. Some post about their holidays and how they are having a good time. Take notice of how people respond when they receive a new notification on their mobile phones.

You may be forgiven for thinking that a bomb has been dropped in front of them, judging by how quickly they react to the beep of the message! I must emphasise that this is not only limited to Facebook; it happens with all the other social media platforms and WhatsApp too. This is a serious challenge, because more and more time is spent on social media.

You need to create your daily routines and stick to them to avoid being bombarded by these distractions. Be more aware of potential risks such as Facebook depression so that you don't fall prey to the lure of spending excessive time on social media. You may be brilliantly efficient at using social media, but if you don't benefit from it, you're wasting your time and wasting your life. You're not being effective. Remember that to achieve your dreams, you need to be both effective and efficient. You need to be doing the right things to the best of your ability most of the time.

By the way, I have nothing against social media. Obviously, if you benefit from social media and most of your work revolves around it, you can and must spend lots of time on it. I dedicate some of my day to updating my social media and, as you probably know, I distribute inspirational pieces via social media.

According to a study by Case Western Reserve University and Florida State University, humans have a finite amount of mental energy for exerting self- control. This means you can make a certain number of good decisions a day and that's that.

You must have heard that both Mark Zuckerberg (the co-founder of Facebook) and Tony Hsieh (Zappos' CEO) wear the same clothes most of the time. They obviously have a few of the same t-shirts and pants in their wardrobes that they wear day in and day out – they don't want to waste a decision on, "What should I wear today?" when they could be working on better things.

It seems rather extreme for the rest of us, doesn't it? But let's learn from them that to be effective and efficient we must spend our precious time on things that add value to our lives.

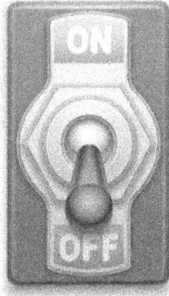

Flip that switch
Action Steps

> **Step 1**

Analyse your morning ritual and make changes where necessary.

My morning ritual is:

My morning will be:

> **Step 2**

Consciously monitor how much time you spend on distractions throughout the day. Make changes where necessary.

My distractions are:

From now onwards, I will:

> **Step 3**

Consciously decide to spend your time on things that add value to your life. These things add value to my life and I here and now decide to spend time on them

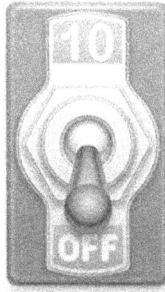

Creative visualisation

"Eyes can see widely; they can cross a river in full flood."
– Old African proverb

Whether you want more, better or different in your professional, personal or sporting life, visualisation can accelerate the achievement of your goals and take you to the next level.

Apparently, Pelé (the Brazilian who is regarded as being the greatest soccer player so far) had the habit of arriving early for a match. He would grab two towels, roll one towel up and use it as a pillow, and put the other over his eyes. Then he would lie down somewhere in the locker room where he could be quiet and he'd do some creative visualisation.

He would imagine he was a kid on the beach doing what he loved most, playing soccer. He would feel the joy and love he had for playing soccer. He would imagine some of his greatest moments and his greatest performances throughout his career.

He would feel it and see it. He would then imagine the game he was about to play and imagine transferring the love he had as a kid and the great performances of the past, into the day's match. He would do that for about half an hour and then hop up and step into the arena – and be unstoppable.

If you want to be unstoppable like Pelé, try creative visualisation.

Visualisation is an internal representation; we internally represent what it is that we want to achieve. This is where you visualise yourself standing on the podium having won some sort of competition. To correctly and effectively visualise, we use three ways in which to experience what is happening: see, hear, and feel. This means that you must firstly see, hear and feel the intangible in your mind as if it is happening in front of you already, so that you take action and behave in a way that is going to make it tangible. This is turning the invisible into the visible, which is what creative visualisation is all about. It starts by being conscious and deliberate.

Here is something to always remember: the subconscious mind can't tell the difference between what is real and what is imagined, it really cannot make the distinction between a mental thought and a physical action. To the subconscious mind they are the same. That is why visualisation is so important and why it works.

Now I am going to ask you to play along as best as you can, because I want you to experience this phenomenon, rather than just read about it.

I am sure that you have had a nightmare at least once in your life where you had to fight or run for your life to survive, woke up screaming and kicking and with your heart racing, only to realise that it was all just a dream. Why would you be so physically involved when you were sleeping and dreaming? This shows that the subconscious can't make a distinction between a dream (something imagined) and something real.

Imagine that you have a lemon in your right hand. It is cut in half, so that you can see the open part and you get that fresh lemon smell, just focus on that smell... ah. Now, bring that lemon up and as you bring it up, just put your lips over the end and suck the juice out, right now. If you are like me, you are going to experience that sour taste sensation, that citric sharpness.

Now imagine you have a piece of rough sandpaper in front of you. Pick up that sandpaper and fold it in half so that the roughness is on the outer sides, and then bring it up to your mouth and put it in between your top and bottom teeth and then move your teeth on the sandpaper. This is even worse than the lemon juice to be honest – it gives you goose bumps.

Finally, think of a relaxing holiday that you recently enjoyed. Think of what you saw, how you felt and what you did. Drop into that feeling and you'll start relating to that wonderful feeling.

The reason you responded the way you did in all these exercises is simply because the subconscious mind can't differentiate between a real or imagined event. Just imagining a lemon creates a physiological result, just like the sandpaper.

The imagined object or scenario creates a physiological response. This is powerful because we can either use this to our advantage, or allow it to be used against us.

One of the biggest mistakes people make is that they talk about and visualise what they don't want. I don't want to be broke anymore... I don't want to be overweight anymore... They are focusing on what they don't want and they are dropping the picture of something they don't want down into the subconscious mind. With that principle in mind, we attract that result that we don't want.

The first key here is to focus on what you want, that is really important. Train yourself to talk and think about what you do want and act consistently with what you do want.

You also have to be in the right state of mind in order to be able to access the power of your mind (harnessing alpha brainwaves is key to unlocking the power of creative visualisation). Before you move on, let's go through the types of brainwaves that produce the various states of mind.

It is important to know that all humans display five different types of electrical patterns or 'brainwaves' across the cortex. The five types of brainwaves are gamma, beta, alpha, theta and delta. The brainwaves can be observed with an EEG (or an electroencephalograph) – a tool that allows researchers to note brainwave patterns. Each brainwave has a purpose and helps serve us in optimal mental functioning.

The extent to which our brains are able to become flexible and to transition through various brainwave frequencies plays a large role in how successful we are at managing stress, focusing on tasks, and getting a good night's sleep.

When one of the five types of brainwaves is either overproduced and/or under produced in our brain, problems can arise. For this reason, it is important to understand that there is no single brainwave that is better or more optimal than the others.

Each serves a purpose to help us cope with various situations – whether it is to help us process and learn new information or help us calm down after a long stressful day. Throughout the day in your waking state, your EEG (electroencephalograph) will display all five types of brainwaves at the same time. However, one particular brainwave will be dominant, depending on the state of consciousness that you are in. For example, if you are awake, but have really bad ADHD (Attention Deficit Hyperactivity Disorder) you will have problems paying attention and probably have more slow wave (alpha and/or theta) activity than beta waves.

When we fall asleep, a large number of neurons in our brain tend to fire in synchronicity resulting in the production of high amplitude delta waves in the brain. There are usually combinations of the slower frequencies during sleep, but even gamma has been found to be involved in rapid- eye movement (REM). Below is a brief description of each brainwave state, but a more in-depth understanding can be derived from the book 'Getting Started With Neurofeedback' by John N. Demos.

Gamma waves

Gamma waves correspond to moments of ecstasy and high energy states in which focus and concentration are at their highest levels. They are considered to be the fastest wave types with frequency ranging from 40 to 100 Hertz. However, our brain seldom shows gamma activity and usually it works in the frequency range associated with beta, alpha, theta and delta waves.

Frequency range	40 Hz to 100 Hz (Highest)
Too much	Anxiety, high arousal, stress
Too little	ADHD, depression, learning disabilities
Optimal	Binding senses, cognition, information processing, learning, perception, REM (rapid-eye movement) sleep.
Increase gamma waves by	Meditation

Beta waves

These high frequency waves, 12 to 40 Hertz are produced in the brain when we are fully involved in some kind of mental activity. This happens when we are in a state of complete alertness and totally focused on the task at hand. A strongly engaged mind is the hallmark of people who spend their time in a beta state. Having an active conversation, playing sports, giving a presentation or attending a job interview requires you to be in a state of increased alertness, which has been associated with the production of beta waves. When there is a dominance of beta wave activity, the mind is sharp and the person is able to think fast and come up with new ideas quickly. The stimulation of beta waves increases our concentration and problem solving ability, which in turn helps improve our peak performance.

Frequency range	12 Hz to 40 Hz (High)
Too much	Adrenaline, anxiety, high arousal, inability to relax, stress
Too little	ADHD, daydreaming, depression, poor cognition
Optimal	Conscious focus, memory, problem solving
Increase beta waves by	Coffee, energy drinks, various stimulants

Alpha waves

These waves travel in the range of 8 to 12 Hertz. This corresponds to relaxation and a sense of calm and well-being. Generating the alpha wave pattern is an indication of a semi-conscious state; the person is neither sleepy nor attentive about his or her surrounding environment. For instance, just after finishing an assigned task we tend to be in a relaxed state of mind, which is the alpha state. During this pleasant alpha break, you may prefer to watch TV, take a short walk in the backyard or simply sit and think over new ideas to resolve an existing issue. The alpha state is relaxing, but at the same time may prompt us to come up with innovative solutions to challenging problems.

Frequency range	8 Hz to 12 Hz (Moderate)
Too much	Daydreaming, inability to focus, too relaxed
Too little	Anxiety, high stress, insomnia, OCD

Optimal	Relaxation
Increase alpha waves by	Alcohol, some antidepressants

Theta waves

These waves are slower than alpha waves and their frequency varies from 4 to 8 Hertz. We often enter this relaxed state of consciousness while performing a repetitive activity such as having a shower, brushing our teeth, watering plants or driving on the same route every day to reach the office. All these activities are monotonous.

They make us feel calm and so we tend to mentally drift to a slower state of theta brainwave activity. Theta waves are also generated while daydreaming, fantasising, imagining and during intuitive thinking. Some of your best creative ideas may pop up in your mind while in this theta state. In this state, the mind disengages itself from reality and focuses more on imaginative thinking.

Frequency range	4 Hz to 8 Hz (Slow)
Too much	ADHD, depression, hyperactivity, impulsivity, inattentiveness
Too little	Anxiety, poor emotional awareness, stress
Optimal	Creativity, emotional connection, intuition, relaxation
Increase theta waves by	Depressants

Delta waves

These waves are the lowest frequencies, ranging between 0 and 4 Hertz, and signify unconscious state of being. No wonder a person in a deep sleep shows delta wave activity in the brain; those high amplitude slow frequency waves are emitted when we are in deep sleep. The production of the delta wave pattern is marked by total loss of awareness that allows the body and the brain to heal. Delta waves help revitalize the brain and are also referred to as healing frequencies. This delta wave pattern has also been detected in deeper meditative states.

Frequency range	0 Hz to 4 Hz (Slowest)
Too much	Brain injuries, learning problems, inability to think, severe ADHD
Too little	Inability to rejuvenate body, inability to revitalize the brain, poor sleep
Optimal	Immune system, natural healing, restorative / deep sleep
Increase delta waves by	Depressants, sleep

Note that the waves that our brains emit are nothing but electrical signals generated when neurons are firing messages to one another. The brain has approximately 80 to 100 billion neurons, specialised cells that communicate with each other by transmitting electrical impulses through neural connections. The quicker the neurons fire at the same time, the higher the frequency of waves. The more the neurons fire synchronously the higher will be the amplitude of the wave.

Although the beta waves are generated often during the day, it doesn't mean the other brainwaves are absent. When one type of brainwave is dominant, the rest are feeble, but continue to be detected. So, the brain produces all waves at all times. Only the strength of the signal will vary depending upon the type of activity we are engaged in.

Brainwaves at a glance

Gamma	Inspiration - Focus - Higher Learning
Beta	Alertness - Concentration - Action
Alpha	Relaxation - Visualization - Creativity
Theta	Meditation - Intuition - Memory
Delta	Healing - Sleep - Cosmic Awareness

Source: http://www.thetawavesforsuccess.com/theta-waves-for-success/ brain-waves-music-alpha-theta-waves-gamma-beta/

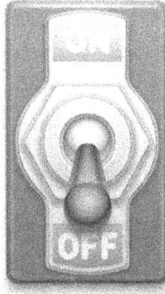

Flip that switch
Action Steps

Let me introduce you to the fun process of creative visualisation (you can't go through this process when you're stressed out). There are five basic steps to this process:

➢ **Step 1**
First decide what you want to achieve or become. Then state your decision/ goal clearly in one short sentence and get a picture of it (wherever possible) so that you can see it.

➢ **Step 2**
Most people try to set goals in the wrong state of mind. It's really important that you relax and get into a relaxed alpha state. The quickest way to get into this state of mind is to think of the most relaxed holiday or outing you had.

Think about what you were seeing, hearing, feeling that made you more relaxed. This immediately puts you in an alpha state, a more relaxed state.

Another way of quickly getting into a relaxed state is to take deep diaphragmatic breaths (about ten of them should be enough). The alpha or relaxed state is the mechanism for forging a bridge between conscious and subconscious minds.

➢ **Step 3**

Imagine and feel your goal. Imagine that you are standing on a podium after achieving what you set out to achieve and that you are seeing a large audience in front of you, smiling at you. See them applaud for you and hear the applause. Feel the feeling of standing on that podium, the feeling of success and achievement. That is the feeling that builds belief and certainty. This means the subconscious mind begins to believe that it is possible.

Now 'float' out of yourself and imagine that you are sitting in the audience and seeing yourself up on the podium with both your hands raised in celebration. This is all about building desire; about looking at an individual and saying, "Oh my goodness! That would be so fantastic to achieve that, what a wonderful achievement." That builds desire.

For this imagination process to work properly, you need to imagine both perspectives (from within yourself and from outside), in order to create belief as well as desire. Next, you'll be adding emotion to the mix – the feeling of success and achievement. This is where the turbo booster comes in and what visualisation is all about. This is where you get to experience the feeling you can expect to experience one day when you finally achieve your goal.

There are two ways to do that. The first is to have your eyes closed and talk yourself through the visualisation. This is talking as if you have already achieved your goal, this will build the feelings: "I am standing on the podium, looking at the audience. They are giving me a big round of applause and cheering me on because I have achieved my goal."

The second and more effective way to do this is to act as if. The reason I wanted you to imagine the lemon and sandpaper in the exercise we did earlier was to specifically make you act as if. I have found that this approach brings out or evokes the feelings of accomplishment so much quicker.

You may have noticed that sports stars who are on top of their game, particularly in tennis or golf, often first visualise themselves achieving their goal by practising their moves ahead of taking their real shot at the ball. In this way, the physical act will evoke the feeling much easier and quicker.

➢ **Step 4**
Before you open your eyes, it's really important that you focus on being the ideal person to achieve the goal. See yourself handling the problems, challenges, difficulties. When it comes to the old habits that used to prevent you from achieving a goal, see yourself handling them better.

See yourself eating what you should be eating and behaving the way you should be behaving. Don't worry too much about reaching that achievement, rather focus on being the person you need to be to achieve it. This is about focusing on the process rather than the end result. This approach will make a huge difference in your life.

➢ Step 5

Repeat the process again and again. Repetition is the mother of all skill. You have to build this into your daily ritual. You have to visualise what it is that you want more than just once a day. If you imagine at least twice a day for five minutes, you drop the images down to your subconscious mind. After seven days you will have done it 14 times – and that will make a huge difference in your behaviour.

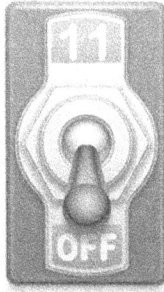

Busy-ness

"A person who chases two rabbits catches neither."
– Confucius (551 BC – 479 BC), Chinese teacher, editor, politician, and philosopher

While chasing a rabbit in the hope of catching it is a difficult task, it certainly gets tougher when a second rabbit is included in the chase. And what do you do when the two rabbits separate and go in different directions? You'll probably end up going straight when one goes left and the other goes right – and you won't catch anything!

The other day, a friend of mine told me about a park in Benoni, where rabbits and baby rabbits (bunnies) roam free. It is apparently very popular with families. People can feed the cute fluffy animals and, of course, try to catch them. She used to go there often when her boys were little. 'I'd even take with them as many of their friends as could fit in the car," she told me. "I'd sit and relax on a bench under a tree while the kids chased the bunnies. The chasing kept them busy the whole, whole day!

They ran around like crazy, in circles round and around the little agile creatures and by the time we went home, they'd be so exhausted that they'd all fall asleep in the car. It was wonderful, the best way for kids to stay busy, get rid of their energy and get fresh air at the same time. And by the way, nobody ever managed to catch a single bunny ever!"

Many of us are like that – we keep ourselves busy running around in circles and not achieving anything, not catching the proverbial bunny. We are spread too thin, taking on more than we can handle, trying to do lots and lots

– almost as if we are afraid that if we were to take a moment of rest, we might discover that all our busy-ness is covering up an essential lack in our lives. This busy-ness tends to become an addiction.

The rabbit conundrum is an illustration of a failure to decide. The word 'decide' has the same Latin root as scissors and incision – to cut. In this case, you are cutting off debate and selecting one of the options available to you, and cutting off the other roots. In short, you commit your focus and your action to the path you have chosen. If you aren't certain, if you have not committed, if your decision is not firm, you face a rabbit dilemma. What will you do when a new option opens up? You will have to make another decision, and lose time, and probably lose both opportunities. Stay focused on your rabbit, or you will forever be chasing and never catching. It is important that you discover the difference between the real work you need to do and the complimentary work that is not essential.

Tim Cook of Apple says that Apple is the most focused company in the world because every day its employees say no to great ideas in order to put enormous energy behind the ones they choose.

The more ideas we choose, the less energy we can put into any single one of them. At the end of the day, in the attention economy where we are surrounded by many voices, many things, many opportunities and so much information, what do we notice? We don't notice the regular, we don't notice the sensible, we don't notice the person who's doing the hard work, we don't notice people who are differentiated, people who stand out, people that are doing things differently. It's clear that if we don't decide to ignore certain things, we will not be able to notice a lot of things in life. When we focus on less things with more thought and more imagination, we get more done and we achieve more.

Never mind rabbits, do you know there's a fish called Siamese fighting fish (commonly known as betta fish). If you put too much food in its bowl, the fish literally eats itself to death. The problem is not that there's too much food, but that it keeps on choosing to eat. It really can't stop itself from eating; as long as there's food in its bowl, it continues to eat.

My question is, "Are we any different from this fish?" We find ourselves constantly having too much to deal with. We are always online. Television, cellular phones and social media platforms, radio, music, computer and TV games have taken over our lives. We are hooked on activity and stimulation. It's so unfortunate because it seems like the majority of us are trapped in busy-ness and noise.

There's too much information to deal with and we are overwhelmed and very busy. This constant overload of information is not getting any better, it's getting worse in fact and this is evidenced by the Knowledge Doubling Curve discovery by Richard Fuller.

Richard Buckminster "Bucky" Fuller was an American architect, systems theorist, author, designer, and inventor. He noticed that until 1900 human knowledge doubled approximately every century. By the end of World War II (1945), knowledge was doubling every 25 years. For example, nanotechnology knowledge is doubling every two years and clinical knowledge every 18 months. But on average human knowledge is doubling every 13 months. According to IBM, the build out of the "internet of things" will lead to the doubling of knowledge every 12 hours.

And the pace of change is unprecedented

Knowledge Doubling Curve
- 1900s, Knowledge doubled every century
- 1940s, knowledge doubled every 25 years
- Currently, knowledge doubling every 13 months
- By 2020, every 12 hours?

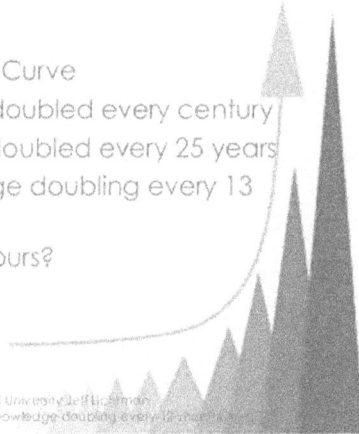

Source: Buckminster Fuller and IBM, Harvard University, Jeff Lickerman, http://www.futuristgerd.com/2014/07/16/knowledge-doubling-every-12-months-to-be-every-12-hours-via-industry-tap/

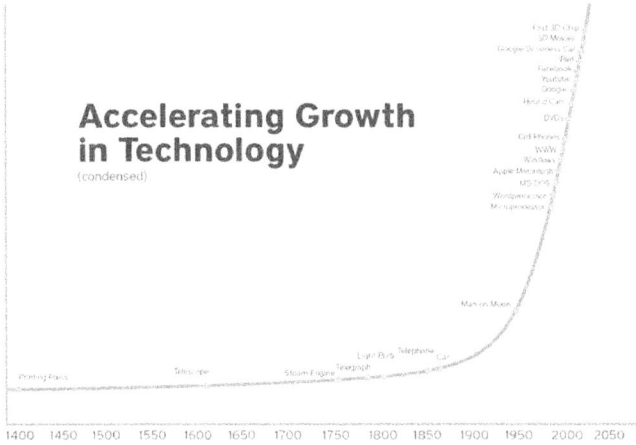

Accelerating Growth in Technology
(condensed)

Source: https://www.webolutions.com/denver-executives-seek-stay-ahead-curve/accelerating-growth-in-technology/

The above graph depicts the accelerating growth (knowledge) in technology between 1400 and 2018.

Whether or not these facts and figures are true (and how they determine what constitutes "doubling" is something I haven't investigated yet), the indisputable fact is that human knowledge is advancing at an extraordinary pace. Medical advances alone are staggering, as well as advances in personal electronics. A transition from the linear growth of human knowledge to the exponential growth of human knowledge has taken place. According to researchers, dealing with this load of knowledge and information will necessitate the development of vastly more complex software, shareability, and artificial intelligence.

Gone, forgotten, or dismissed, is the knowledge (the true knowledge) and skills that allowed mankind to thrive for 5,000-plus years of civilization. How to build a home from raw materials. How to make a fire without matches. How to hunt animals with only the most primitive of tools. How to make those primitive tools. How to raise crops, harvest them and preserve them through the upcoming year. The list of skills we've forgotten is endless.

Our knowledge may be doubling, but our skills are halving. Throw away most peoples' smartphones, put them in a field of ripe wheat next to a lactating cow, and they'll starve to death because they don't know how to milk the cow. We are more helpless and ignorant than we've ever been in the history of humanity. Surprisingly, we are the busiest of all generations, but least productive.

We find ourselves chasing many rabbits and yet catching none. By sharing all this information, especially about the Knowledge Doubling Curve, I hope to help you realise that we have a real focus problem. We need to claim back our focus. By focusing on what matters most, you will be able to do less, be less busy.

Big success comes when you do a few things well versus trying to do too much. You only have a limited amount of time and energy, so when you spread yourself thin, you end up accomplishing too little. Extraordinary results are directly determined by how narrow you make your focus. The main key to success is to narrow it down to one very important thing.

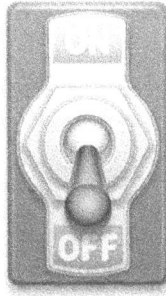

Action Steps

> **Step 1**

Right now, reflect on the following myths and lies that keep us busy, and not achieving much:

1. **Everything matters equally:** This is the thinking that there is so much to be done, I am so overworked; I am over-committed and I am over expended; there's too much... In the world of results, things are never equal, there can't be x number of things of equal importance that need to be done simultaneously. There's always one thing that's more important than other things.

   High achievers understand that not all things are equal. High achievers have a clear sense and work from a clear sense of priority. They find the one thing that's the most important and they let that drive their day. They realise that the things that are the most important are not the things that scream the loudest or that are urgent.

Activity is often unrelated to productivity and it's key to understand that success is not a game that is won by whoever does the most. We tend to assume that the person who is the busiest, most active and who puts the most effort is the person that will become the most successful – it often doesn't work like that.

Successful people mostly work on 80/20 principle which asserts that a minority of causes, inputs or efforts usually lead to a majority of results, outputs or rewards. Your critical responsibility is to identify the 20% that will yield 80% of your results, that's very important. You can even go narrower by applying 80/20 of the 20% until you reach the one most important thing.

Doing the one essential thing is a lot more productive than trying to do everything. Doing the most important thing is the most important thing. Write down your to do list and prioritise the tasks, starting off with the most important thing and then the next one and so on. Focus on following a rational sequence.

2. **Multitasking:** This is the thinking that you'll get more done by doing things at the same time. This doesn't really help at all. Multitasking is also seen as a strength by most people, which is a very unfortunate thing. If doing the most important thing is the most important thing, why would you try doing anything else at the same time?
    Just do the most important thing, period. Focusing on two different things at once reduces your attention and the things you are focusing on won't get the attention they deserve.

This is like spreading water across many plants and none of the plants gets enough water to grow. Eventually they die or grow weak. There is just so much brain capability at any one time; you can divide it   as much as you want, but you will end up paying the price in time and effectiveness.

Bouncing from task to task will waste your time as your brain re-orients itself to the new task and may lead you to believe that tasks take longer to complete than is actually required. Every time you switch activities, your brain needs to re-wire and you lose that deep focus.

Say you are fully engaged doing some serious writing and the notifier pops up on your screen. You glance to Facebook for a few seconds and lose your focus. When you get back to your writing, it'll take you a few minutes or so to really get back into it. This means that something that could have been done in a short period of time just gets dragged out – and the quality suffers and you end up feeling horrible.

It's best to switch off your phone and email notifiers and all other external distractions so you can immerse yourself into deep engagement with your task at hand.
A lot of the things you think are urgent, are not important nor urgent. You can select precise times when to check texts; discipline yourself to check your emails only every once in a while. Most people, unfortunately feel like it would be the end of the world if they don't check their emails or messages every minute.

The idea here is to make tough choices; of making important trade-offs. Stop managing time and start managing activities.

This will enable you to move from surface layer attention, being scattered all over the place from different social media notifications to deep attention. The opposite of busy is not relaxation, but a sustained focus, did you know? Deep thinking versus scattered thinking.

Perfection is really an illusion, you will never attain it in this world of ours. Accept the fact that there's always and will always be too much and your responsibility is to choose the most important things to focus on and do so well. Get used to having unopened emails and unanswered messages.

Most people can't stand this, they feel like they have to always read and clear all messages and emails, no, it's okay to trade some of them with more important things. You can leave your phone off every once in a while.

Basically, you can't do it all and you shouldn't do it all! Let go of control and the thought that you should be on top of everything. So, if you are constantly busy, it's because you are not making the right choices.
You're still trying to do everything instead of doing the right things. Life is about making the right choices and this is the muscle that you build.

To have greater focus on fewer things, pick the important ones and immerse yourself in them. The question you should be asking yourself is not whether or not to do things, but which do you prefer doing; this will force you to prioritise. Which of the things in front of you will benefit you the most? Decide what matters most and focus on the most important thing.

> ➢ **Step 2**

Right now, if you look at your day, there's probably a whole lot of tasks that need to be done. List them and choose the most important ones. You can't do all of them. You only have limited time, energy, attention and willpower and to ensure they are used wisely, you must focus on the important tasks.

When you see someone who is successful, you tend to assume that they became successful without much effort and that they are better and more disciplined than you are. In reality, successful people are not any better than you and me.

Somewhere along their lives, they invested loads of effort in creating good habits, relationships and building self-discipline. They learnt about prioritising important things.

Your job is to build the right habits. Success is about one right thing, not about doing everything right. Choose the right habit and bring enough discipline to establish it and then move on to the next one.

> ➢ **Step 3**

Most people feel overwhelmed by the number of choices they have. We have this fear of missing out on things. We have this astonishing fear of loss maybe as fed by the social media, maybe as fed by all the information that we get about the different choices and options we have.

We need to learn that more options aren't necessarily a good thing. The fact is, we can't do everything. The more you try to do, the less focus each task gets and the less joy you get out of it.

We spend most of our time looking forward to the next thing rather than being present in the moment. Kill FOMO (Fear Of Missing Out) right now. Every time you feel FOMO rise up from inside you, kill it. It's only a feeling, you can kill it! Do it.

Step 4
Life is like a buffet table, it's full of things on it and it's very tempting to have most of those things and not miss out on anything. How can you choose one thing above the other? Ask yourself, "Which of the options available right now is the right one? Which will give me joy and benefit me the most?" Asking 'which' a few times takes you closer to a better choice. Choosing one is difficult. Actually, the busier we are, the more we tend to choose more. Right now, ask yourself the which question – and choose one thing to do next.

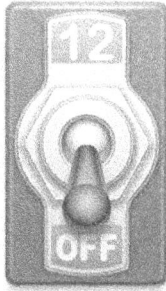

Power talk

"Feeling sorry for yourself, and your present condition, is not only a waste of energy but the worst habit you could possibly have."
– Dale Carnegie (1888 –1955), American developer of famous courses salesmanship and interpersonal skill, author of bestselling book 'How to Win Friends and Influence People'

Think of your brain as a super-computer and your self-talk as a program that runs on it. This means that you always need to monitor your self-talk, that's very important. If you tell yourself you are not good at something, your statement will be validated. So, keep your self-talk positive; keep it empowering because your mind is always eavesdropping on your self-talk.

Self-development superstar Dr Wayne Dyer (now deceased), the author of 'Your Erroneous Zones' (1976) coined the famous phrase, "I'll see it when I believe it". It stands in stark contrast to "I'll believe it when I see it."
Top achievers approach life in this manner; they constantly go against the common thinking.

To believe something before you see it shows that for anything to exist, it must be created twice – first in the mind and then in the physical world.

Consider that until 1954, athletes and people alike believed that it was impossible to run a mile in under four minutes. Then UK athlete Roger

Bannister came along and broke the four-minute mile record. Shortly after that, other athletes started running the mile below four minutes – this was not due to a change in training methodology and nutrition, but due to a change in belief. It's awesome isn't it? It's been proven over and again that once you do something you have never done before, you open yourself to new possibilities.

You can even change your identity. Because your identity is who you believe you are, you can change your identity by using the two small words, 'I am'. These two words are powerful because whatever you put after them determines your destiny. Say, "I am positive", and surely enough you will start feeling more positive.

Some successful people are known to have experienced tough situations which could have resulted in Post-Traumatic Stress Disorder (PTSD).
Yet they managed to turn misfortune around and transformed PTSD into Post Traumatic Growth (PTG). They found new meaning in their lives, new levels of commitment and wouldn't trade their painful experiences for anything in the world. These are the likes of Nelson Mandela, Victor Frankl, Opera Winfrey, Maya Angelou and many others.

While testing the "Believing is seeing" theory, you may also want to reflect on the following lessons from top performers:

- **Run your own race:** This means you must recognise that you were born for a reason. There was an empty space that your maker saw in the world and created you to fill it. He didn't create you to be like others. So, stay in your own lane. You have no competition if you are in your own division. It's so easy to be swept off your game, swept off your vision, swept off your values and swept off your focus when you are measuring your performance and success by other people's standards.

  Running your own race is a profound principle that you need to remember at all times. Come up with your own vision and ambition and focus on it with great discipline as if your life depends on it. This will help you stay true to yourself and keep you focused on measuring your success in terms of how close you are getting to your mountain top versus the mountain top of others.

- **Strive to be the best you:** As you do this, always remember that there are great people who can help you get started at a higher level and save time re-inventing the wheel. Isaac Newton, the greatest mathematician said, "If I can see further, it is by standing on the shoulders of giants." Identify world-class leaders in your field and study their rituals and behaviour. You can't be casual and expect to be world class; you need laser-like focus, deliberate and deep work. To raise your game means you have to raise your standards. You also have to learn to switch off from all the external distractions and focus on your craft. It's important to know that genius is less about inherited genetics and much more about your installed habits.

- **Be willing to be eccentric:** You can choose to be like the majority of people (the 95%) or play in rare air and be in the minority (the 5%) – you can't do both. If you choose to play in rare air, you have to adopt a different mind-set, heart-set and skill-set and this will make you unpopular and at times confused.

  The sad reality is that 95% of people 'coast' through their lives, it's a silent majority that has lost the fire in their bellies, watching too much TV, self-medicating with too much gossip and lost in the busy-ness of the world – busy being busy.
  The 95% is on silent pain of the potential unexpressed and they think it's okay. As you shift from the majority and rise to the rare air where the 5% lives, you will have to think and feel differently and install different rituals. It means you will have to be somewhat eccentric. You have to develop courage and character that enables you to handle being ridiculed, mocked and laughed at, as you take your new path. Please, remember that every great genius and leader was once misunderstood and made fun of, don't let this deter you!

- **Deep work:** Dr Cal Newport wrote a book entitled 'Deep Work'. The only place to monopolise your industry is to be deep in what you do. Don't just be light, you have to be deep! Don't just share things that are known by everybody in the industry; come up with something novel. You have to be so good at what you do, that when people watch you in action, tears come to their eyes and they rise to their feet and applaud you.

This can only happen if you separate yourself from how most people operate in business and in life, therefore go deep. We are living in a world where superficiality is fashionable, everything is fast and light. Resolve today to go deep when working on a project, building a client relationship, interacting with people and in all things that matter. Resolve to have substance and to go beyond the superficial.

Success requires positive self-talk as well as lots of hard work behind the scenes. A successful person is like a duck in a pond: it may appear calm and relaxed on the surface but under the surface of the water, the duck is hustling really fast.

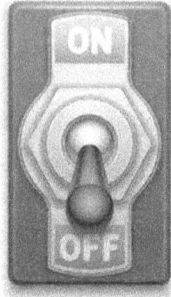

Flip that switch

Action Steps

> **Step 1**

Write down an evidence list, that is a list (in bullet points) of everything you have done in your life that shows something good about you (caring, honest) / that you've experienced or achieved (a diploma) / that provides evidence of your strengths (overcame an obstacle). Have you mentored anyone formally and informally? Have you created anything artistic in music, graphics, etc? Have you ever managed a project, visited the sick or helped out in the community? Have you ever responded to an emergency situation with courage and clarity of thought?

Evidence list:

> **Step 2**

Write down a strengths list; the list below should help you remember your good qualities and you can add others as well.

IMPULSIVE RESPONSIBLE EFFICIENT CONFIDENT ENERGETIC

COMPASSIONATE FUNNY

KIND DIPLOMATIC RELAXED

CARING METICULOUS ORGANIZED OUTGOING

FOLLOW THROUGH ON THINGS INTUITIVE TEAM PLAYER CHARMING

LEVELHEADED OBSERVANT REALIABLE OPEN-MINDED PATIENT

DECISIVE

DRIVEN INTELLIGENT CHARISMATIC IMAGINATIVE ADVENTUROUS

LOYAL PEOPLE PERSON CREATIVE ENTHUSIASTIC

PERSUASIVE EASYGOING

COMMANDING PASSIONATE

PUNCTUAL ARTICULATE GENEROUS

TAKE INITIATIVE CURIOUS

SENSITIVE EMPHATHETIC OPTIMISTIC

FOCUSED PERSISTENT CLEVER

Strengths list:

> Step 3
> Write down a passion list; look back on all of the things that you listed in the evidence section and ask yourself, "In which of these things that I was involved in, was I truly happy? In which did I lose myself in? In which did I feel that I had a talent but that talent was growing, developing and expanding and giving me immense pleasure whilst giving tremendous value to the world?" If you can answer these questions you will be hitting on the second key ingredient which will empower you with action: passion. Whatever you are truly passionate about will help you reach a state which has been termed 'flow'.

Flow, a state which has been exhaustively written about and lectured on by Mihaly Csikszentmihalyi, has been shown to have a huge connection to our happiness levels. The state involves such an immersion in the activity which you feel skilled in and passionate about that you transcends into the activity itself. As a result, you feel you have no needs and wants in those moments. It seems that a huge amount of pleasure is connected with the fact that many of your human needs are being fulfilled at once.

Passion list:

> **Step 4**

American basketball coach Tim Notke said, "Hard work beats talent when talent doesn't work hard." There are ten things that require zero talent and when done well, success will be unavoidable. Memorise the list below and apply to your everyday life:
1. being on time
2. having a good work ethic
3. giving your best effort
4. having high energy
5. smiling and having good body language
6. being optimistic and having a great attitude
7. having passion
8. being-coachable
9. doing more than expected
10. being prepared

> **Step 5**

Decide which you'd rather be – a thermometer or a thermostat? The thermometer reflects what the environment is giving it. It reflects the temperature. But the thermostat is different; it sets a standard; it sets a goal; it sets a vision and the environment changes along with it.

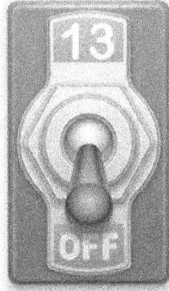

The seven universal laws

"History, despite its wrenching pain, cannot be unlived, but if faced with courage, need not be lived again."
– Maya Angelou (1928 – 2014), American poet, singer, memoirist, and civil rights activist

Are things happening to you that leave you puzzled? Are bad things taking place in your life and you have no idea how to change or control them? Are you enjoying good things and you want to know how to keep it that way? If so, you may want to pay close attention to the seven universal laws. These are natural laws as basic as the law of gravity, and, if you use them in the right way, they can help you create what you want out of life. If you pay close attention, you will no longer be able to say, "I don't know why these things happen to me."

Like a car – if you keep it fuelled, oil changed, properly maintained, and properly handled and driven – a life lived in accordance with the laws of the universe will last long and serve you well.

This does not mean that things will not need to be replaced and cared for, but you will have much more success and longevity than otherwise. It also doesn't mean that I'm ignoring the laws of God, the 10 Commandments. Not at all. God created the universe and created us to live in His universe. In my opinion there's no conflict of interest; when we observe the seven universal laws, we indirectly observe the laws of

God the Creator as well. The seven universal laws can be traced back over 7,000 years to the ancients of Egypt, Greece and the Vedic traditions of India so this is not new knowledge. It's ancient wisdom.

Basically, we can be going throughout our day-to-day lives and doing all the things that we are doing and the natural laws will still happen. Note that there is no particular order in the sequence of these laws, meaning there's no first law, second law, third law, and so on.

These seven laws can bring stability, assurance, and confidence to your life if you make the choice of understanding, and applying them. There is a lot of information about these laws in many books and on the Internet. I have made the following summary for ease of understanding:

The Law of Vibration:
   – This law states that everything vibrates and nothing rests. Vibrations of the same frequency resonate with each other, so like attracts like energy. Everything is energy, including your thoughts.

Consistently focusing on a particular thought or idea attracts its vibrational match. This simply means that energy follows intentions. What goes on or happens inside of you is what creates this universe. I am sure you have heard of the saying that we do not attract what we want, but we attract what we are. You are what you think about most of the time.

– To apply this law in your favour: focus on what you want instead of what you don't want. Focusing on what you want will begin to change your frequency and will attract like energy into your life.

The Law of Relativity:
– States that nothing is what it is until you relate it to something. Point of view is determined by what the observer is relating to. The nature, value, or quality of something can only be measured in relation to another object. Nothing is good or bad until you relate it to something. Practice relating your situation to something worse, and yours will always look good. If you practice relating your situation to something better, yours will always look worse. Nothing is good or bad until you relate it to something. Imagine three bank accounts: the first with R150 in it, the second with R150,000, and the third with R150,000,000. None of them are large, and none are small unless you compare them to a larger or smaller account.

– How to apply it in your favour: practise relating your situation to something worse than yours, and you will feel good about where you are. In my case, I compared my story of tragically losing my parents at a young age to Les Brown's story of not even knowing his parents as he and his twin brother were found in an abandoned building.

I realised how lucky I was to have at least known my parents and some special moments I shared with them. This made my situation feel much better as I realised that it wasn't the worst.

The Law of Cause and Effect:
– States that for every action, there's an equal and opposite reaction. Every cause has an effect, and every effect has a cause. All thought is creative, so be careful of what you wish for... you will get it. This means that whatever you put out there, you'll get it back tenfold. If we have bad thoughts about other people or ourselves, it's going to come back again to us. This once again goes back to the Law of Vibration. Always know that if you put ill-will out there, ill-will is going to come back to you. If you put worry out there, worry will come back.

– How to apply it to your advantage: consistently think and act on what you desire to be effective at getting it. If you want love, start by loving yourself first and you will attract it to you. Think of things that bring out passion and that light you up. Whatever you send into the universe comes back. Say good things to everyone; treat everyone with total respect, and it will all come back to you.
Never worry about what you are going to get. Just concentrate on what you can give and give it unconditionally. What goes around comes around. If you squeeze an orange, you will get orange juice. Like causes always produce like effects.

The Law of Polarity:
– States that everything has an opposite. Hot-Cold, Light-Dark, Up- Down, Good-Bad. In the absence of that which you are not, that which you are... is not. Polar opposites make existence possible. If what you are not didn't co-exist with what you are, then what you are couldn't be. Therefore, don't condemn or criticise what you are not or what you don't want. Pay attention to these things that are happening in your life so the law of polarity kicks in. It is there to make us understand all aspects of who we are because when it comes to good and bad, there's good and bad in all of us. We have the capability of doing some pretty horrific things and very wonderful things and so when we understand the light and darkness in us and we dive into our darkness instead of avoiding it.

– How to apply it to your advantage: look for the good in people and situations. What you focus on, you make bigger in your life. If you are upset with people because they betrayed you or because you felt offended, then the universe is going to bring in more people that will offend you because remember, we attract what we are, not what we want.
If you are in a peaceful state, relaxed and somebody is really loud in front of you, that's obviously a polarity. But if you choose to remain still in that situation, the opposite will be true, you won't attract anything that will really upset you.

The Law of Rhythm:
– States that everything has a natural cycle. The tides go in and back out, night follows day, and life regenerates itself. We all have good times and bad times, but nothing stays the same. Change is constant. Knowing that, "This too shall pass" is great wisdom about life's ebb and flow.

Things have happened to you in the past especially the bad ones – but eventually they passed. Whenever you are in this bad and cloudy situation, try to be still and remember similar or even the worst thing like it that happened to you in the past and surely you will feel somehow better remembering that it too passed. Nothing stays forever. Family members are going to be born and also, they are going to die, it's a natural cycle of life. Understand the Law of Polarity, there'salwaystwosidestoacoin. The Law of Rhythm will then follow.

– How to apply it in your favour: when you are on a downswing, know that things will get better. Think of the good times that are coming.

The Law of Gestation:
– States that everything takes time to manifest. All things have a beginning and grow into form as more energy is added to it. Thoughts are like seeds planted in our fertile minds that bloom into our physical experience if we have nourished them.
This is something super important to understand. Practise your craft or an idea that you have and do so over and over and over with the appreciation and understanding that in time, it willmanifest.

– How to apply this in your life: stay focused and know that your goals will become a reality when the time is right. Divine timing in divine order.

The Law of Transmutation:
– States that energy moves in and out of physical form. Your thoughts are creative energy.

The more you focus your thoughts on what you want, the more you harness your creative power to move that energy into results in your life. The universe organises itself according to your thoughts.

How to apply it: put your energy and effort, your thoughts and action into attracting what you desire, and you'll surely attract the physical manifestation of that energy. This energy is limitless and inexhaustible.

These are the seven laws of the universe. The interesting point is that nature is neutral. In other words, nature doesn't care who you are. It doesn't care if you're tall or short, male or female, black or white, educated or uneducated, it really doesn't care. All that nature cares about is that you do what has to be done. It's like a recipe; you follow a recipe exactly, you succeed in making the cake. But if you don't follow the recipe, your cake flops. Nature doesn't care who does the baking.

There are lots of people who are not as smart and not as talented as you, but they are doing much better than you. This is because they're following proven success methods. There's nothing that will make you madder than to see somebody who's dumber than you making more money than you. I am sure you've had that experience before. You need to follow the proven methods for success and do them over and over again.

Here's something I've learnt in my journey to success: nothing works the first time. Research has shown that the average number of times that a person tries with a new goal before they give up is less than one.

One of the easiest things is to find a long list of excuses why you won't do something instead of one reason, a very strong reason as to why you must do it.

Successful people have been studied thoroughly and you can find out everything there is to know about them. The information ranges from where they come from, how they were raised, how they thought, where they started, the decisions they made and also what kind of people they were.

What I personally learned from truly successful people is that becoming a millionaire for example is not the important thing. What is really important is the person you have to become to be worth a million rand. Jim Rohn once said, "In order to achieve something you've never achieved before, you have to become someone you've never been before." This is an important insight you need to have. Think of the qualities that you need to develop over time.

I am sure you've heard of lotto winners who became instant millionaires and lost their millions overnight, as they didn't have the required qualities to keep and grow those millions. Qualities like determination, discipline, decision- making, strength and so on make you a far better person.

Someone once said that if all the money were to be taken out of the rich people's pockets and be equally shared among every person in the world, it would soon be back in the same pockets of the rich people. This proves what I have referred to above that you have to firstly develop the right qualities to have money, keep it and grow it otherwise even if you can have it, you would soon lose it.

I hope you find the seven universal laws helpful. Whether something goes right or something goes wrong, you can refer to these laws.

The people who have not gotten what their heart desires have gone against one or more of these laws. Read and learn all about the laws that affect you on this planet and you're sure to succeed.

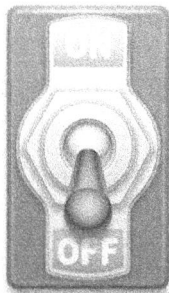

Flip that switch

Action Steps

➢ **Step 1**

Apply the Law of Vibration: focus on what you want instead of what you don't want. Write down:
From this moment on, I want and will focus on:

➢ **Step 2**

Apply the Law of Relativity: practise relating your situation to something worse than yours. Write down:
My situation could be worse, I could be blind/lame or:

➢ **Step 3**

The Law of Cause and Effect: Do and say good things and it will come back to you. Write down:
From this moment on I will say good things to everyone and treat everyone with total respect.
This is what I will Say:
This is what I'll do:

➢ **Step 4**

The Law of Polarity: look for the good in people and situations. Write down:
Right now I see the following good in (name the person/s):
Right now I see the following good in (name the situation):

> ### Step 5
The Law of Rhythm: Look at what's good in your life right now and say, "This too shall pass". Do the same with what's bad in your life right now. Write down:
This too shall pass (good):

This too shall pass (bad):

> ### Step 6
The Law of Gestation: Practise your craft or an idea that you have and do so over and over and over with the appreciation and understanding that in time, it will manifest.

> ### Step 7
The Law of Transmutation: put your energy and effort, your thoughts and action into attracting what you desire, and you'll surely attract the physical manifestation of that energy. Write down:

This is what I desire:
Close your eyes and visualise what you desire.

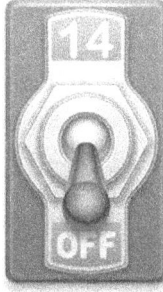

Difficult people

"Whoever walks with the wise becomes wise, but the companion of fools will suffer harm."
– Proverbs 13:20, the Holy Bible

In our day-to-day living, we are forced to interact with countless people who are not necessarily people we would choose to associate with. This includes work colleagues, general public, clients and even family members. All these people have different traits and it's a fact that you aren't going to be able to get on well with everyone. Even the people we love tend to have personality traits that we dislike! It's therefore useful, I discovered, to learn a little about psychology so that you can have meaningful human interactions that provide a positive outcome.

As I have had times in my life when I felt completely bewildered and overwhelmed by certain people, I decided to learn, in particular, about people that have malicious traits.

I've summarised some of the information in the public domain and hope it will be helpful to you. But please bear in mind that I am not a psychologist. I only provide this information here to make you aware that seriously flawed people live and work among us. Let's take a look at the 'Dark Triad Traits', namely narcissism, Machiavellianism and psychopathy.

Narcissism: narcissists essentially take self-confidence to the extreme and view themselves as being perfect beings capable of doing no wrong, all powerful and often with special abilities. Sometimes this will extend into full- blown delusions of grandeur in which they fantasise about perceived abilities or rights.

They will likely see themselves as superior and entitled and so their outward behaviour will often come across as arrogant or condescending. In some cases, this self-importance and sense of superiority will result in their being manipulative and destructive in relationships – doing what they must, to get ahead. They may lack empathy and in extreme cases might be party to abusive relationships.

Another trait of narcissists is attention-seeking behaviour, they're likely to try and grab the spotlight. They will desperately seek approval and adulation for their abilities and achievements and they will react strongly and negatively to criticism (they will also deny any failings and will be adept at constructing excuses and blaming outside sources for their failures). They are highly self-dependent in all other ways (or so it will seem) and they will as a result be likely to be highly secretive and often unsociable.

The secret to understanding narcissists is to understand the 'narcissist's wound', what Freud would call an 'ego defence mechanism'.

The wound can be due to losing someone close to them, or being betrayed by someone they loved. Narcissists use self-love to ensure they don't get hurt again and become reliant on others again.

When dealing with narcissists, keep in mind the narcissistic wound as this can help you be less frustrated by the selfish behaviour. If you recognise that their actions and words are a result of a childhood trauma, then it is easier to be more sympathetic.

However, you need to play 'hardball' with narcissists in order to make sure that you don't let their lack of empathy and delusions damage you. Don't worry about insulting narcissists or trying to bring them back down to earth as they are thick skinned and nothing you say is likely to cause any damage – but it might be enough to make them back off and move on to an easier target. You need to be thick skinned and don't take their put downs to heart; they live in a fantasy world and are unable to make a realistic assessment of you.

Treat them with respect and kindness as you would anyone else. If you want to (and are brave enough), you can help nurture their self-confidence – because remember that deep down they need the encouragement.
However, make sure that you boost their esteem in a way that is congruent with reality

– focus on their real strengths, whether they be artistic or creative or resourcefulness and show them unconditional love that teaches them they don't need to 'act out' when they are around you.

Don't try to change them or 'fix' them, unless you're a trained psychologist and they have specifically requested you to help them change.

Machiavellianism: Niccolo Machiavelli (1469-1527), political philosopher and author of 'The Prince' wrote, "A wise ruler ought never to keep faith when by doing so it would be against his interests," and, "A prince never lacks good reasons to break his promise." According to Machiavelli, honesty – and all other virtues – are expendable if deceit, treachery, and force would be more expedient. In short, he would argue, people in positions of power should choose to be, well, Machiavellian, even if that is not their natural leadership style.

In psychology, Machiavellianism refers to a personality type that does not choose to be, but simply is, a master manipulator. They are temperamentally predisposed to be calculating, conniving, and deceptive. Essentially immoral, they use other people as stepping stones to reach their goals.

We can all be duplicitous at times, depending on need or circumstances. If you've ever called in sick when you were well or lied to your spouse about what you were doing, you have demonstrated the human capacity to con others.
Such episodes probably do not reflect your standard behaviour patterns, and you may have felt a little guilty. But this type of behaviour is routine for Machiavellians.

How can you spot a Machiavellian? Here are four characteristics to watch for:

1. They function best in jobs and social situations where the rules and boundaries are ambiguous.
2. Emotional detachment and a cynical outlook enable them to control their impulses and be careful, patient opportunists.

3. They prefer to use subtle tactics (charm, friendliness, self-disclosure, guilt), when possible, to mask their true intentions and provide a basis for plausible denial if they are detected. However, they can use pressure and threats when necessary.

4. They tend to be preferred by others in competitive situations (debating, negotiations), but are not preferred as friends, colleagues, or spouses.
Those who can be classified as having Machiavellian personalities, will be more likely to manipulate others to get their own ends – to use people in relationships and to happily trample on others to get ahead.

Psychopathy: don't confuse psychopath and sociopath with psychotic. Psychotic means you're seeing elves and unicorns. Psychopaths see the world quite clearly. Perhaps too clearly.
As Ronald Schouten, professor of psychiatry at Harvard Medical School explains, they don't let irritating things like conscience or empathy get in the way. Because they don't possess either of them. Psychopathy is a psychological condition in which the individual shows a profound lack of empathy for the feelings of others, a willingness to engage in immoral and antisocial behaviour for short-term gains, and extreme egocentricity.

No, they don't all have cold, dead eyes and wear a hockey mask. Many are witty and quite articulate. They're narcissistic and impulsive. And because they lack empathy they see other people as objects to be used. Just because they don't feel empathy doesn't mean they don't understand it. And many get quite good at faking it. All the better to manipulate you to get what they want. Neuroscience research shows the emotional centres of their brains don't respond the way yours do.

According to Robert Hare, the criminal psychologist who developed the test used to evaluate psychopaths, many psychopaths never go to prison or any other facility. They appear to function reasonably well – as lawyers, doctors, psychiatrists, academics, mercenaries, police officers, cult leaders, military personnel, businesspeople, writers, artists, entertainers, and so forth – without breaking the law, or at least without being caught and convicted. These individuals are every bit as egocentric, callous, and manipulative as the average criminal psychopath; however, their intelligence, family background, social skills, and circumstances permit them to construct a facade of normalcy and to get what they want with relative impunity.

Hare says that whether subclinical psychopaths are sabotaging your love life or your workplace, they usually follow a three-step process:

1. They assess the utility, weaknesses and defences of those around them
2. They manipulate others to bond with them and get what they want
3. They abandon their targets and move on... Or, in a corporate environment, often move up.

Together with industrial psychologist Paul Babiak, Hare wrote a book called, 'Snakes in Suits: When Psychopaths Go to Work'. The book provides great insights into the mind of psychopaths. Apparently, psychopaths first assess the value of individuals to their needs, and identify their psychological strengths and weaknesses. Second, they manipulate the individuals (now potential victims) by feeding them carefully crafted messages, while constantly using feedback from them to build and maintain control. Not only is this an effective approach to take with most people, it also allows psychopaths to talk their way around and out of any difficulty quickly and effectively if confronted or challenged. Third, they leave the drained and bewildered victims when they are bored or otherwise through with them.

If they invade your personal life, they turn on that artificial empathy and charm. They listen to hear what you think of yourself and reinforce that. The message? I like who you are. Then they pretend they share similar qualities. Message? I am just like you.

Note that none of these traits on their own is enough to make someone a 'bad person' – and even when all three are present, this doesn't always lead to criminal or even truly antisocial behaviour. In fact, there are many psychopaths in positions of power and responsibility – many CEOs, politicians and other prominent figures find themselves rising to the top of their respective hierarchies to take on leadership roles and to bring about a lot of social change, positively for the greater good.

It's also important to note that people exhibiting these traits might find themselves at different points on the spectrum. Many people can be considered a little vain, which is not to say that they're going to make a bid for world domination!

Alright, so you're pretty sure this new person in your life or that new co- worker at the office is manipulative and playing puppet-master. The experts recommend you deal with them as follows:

- Accept that some people are bad news: The first rule involves the bitter pill of accepting that some people literally have no conscience... Do not try to redeem the unredeemable. You can't change them. What you can do is get to know how they work and get to know yourself better. Know where your vulnerabilities lie. Because psychopaths are experts at figuring them out. Address your weaknesses before they exploit them.

- Pay attention to actions, not words: This is another one all the sources agreed on. Don't listen to the excuses, rationalisations or outright lies. Don't listen to what they say they will do. Pay attention to what they do.

- Build your reputation and relationships: The psychopaths at work are always recruiting unsuspecting "patrons" in upper management to unknowingly provide cover for them when rumours about their shady behaviour start to circulate. And they'll also be leveraging these relationships to spread disinformation and lies about anyone who gets in their way or poses a threat. And that might include you.

So, make sure to build your own relationships and keep a reputation as   a hard worker. Be above reproach. Don't be a complainer. That way when you do complain, senior people listen. And if you're dealing with a possible psychopath in your personal life, relationships are just as important. Friends can often be more objective than you can. When multiple confidantes say "He/She is no good", you might want to listen.

- Win-Win agreements: Psychopaths have aggressive personalities. They want to win. If you can make it easier and more enticing for them to work with you than to try to subvert you, you may be able to keep their ruthlessness in check.

   When you bargain with any aggressive personality, try to propose as many win-win scenarios as you can. Doing this is important and requires creativity and a particular mind set. But in my experience, it's perhaps the single most effective personal empowerment tool because it puts to constructive use the aggressive personality's determination to win.

- Now, don't go falling into the trap of playing amateur psychoanalyst, calling everyone who has ever been mean to you a psychopath. But, that said, this is an area where research says you actually might be able to trust your gut.

   Your main goal is to be fair to everyone you meet. At the same time, don't let difficult people do you harm or hold you back.

Flip that switch

Action Steps

➤ **Step 1**

Think about the people that are giving you a hard time at present. Do you think anyone is a narcissist? Machiavellian? Psychopath?

➤ **Step 2**

If the answer is yes, what do you intend doing about it? Write down some tips for yourself:

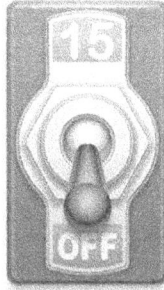

The power of 'why'

"The thinking that got us to where we are is not the thinking that will get us to where we want to be."
– Albert Einstein (1874 – 1955), Jewish physicist who developed the theory of relativity

What worked for us yesterday won't necessarily work for us today and tomorrow. And the reason why most of us are stuck today is simply because we are still using yesterday's technique and approach to solve today's problems though it's no longer enough or applicable.

The Law of Cause and Effect (which is touched on in chapter 13) explains that almost every result we produce (effect) is a result of what we do (cause), knowingly or unknowingly. Furthermore, the reason you do what you do, has a major impact on the quality of the results you produce. Why do you eat? Think about it; what are your reasons for eating? My reasons are:

- To fill my hungry tummy
- To stay alive
- To get energy and fuel my body cells with the nutrients they need Just as a power station requires gas or coal to power its turbines and generate energy, so we need fuel – in the form of food – to power our continued existence.

The foods we eat provide us with a range of nutrients: vitamins, minerals, water, fat, carbohydrates, fibre, and protein. These nutrients are put to different uses as building materials to construct the tissues and organs from which our bodies are made.

If your reason for eating is to fill an emotional void, you will probably end up overeating and putting on weight. If you eat purely out of habit, without thinking about what you're eating, you will probably end up eating food that doesn't have nutritional value – and consequently feel run down and have no energy.

Why do you go to school? Think about it; what are your reasons for going to school? My reasons were:
- Because everybody goes to school
- To get more knowledge about things o To get a better job
- To discover my strengths and talents o Because it's a legal requirement

We go to school to gain education. Education is the ability to think and think through what the books are teaching us; think through what the teachers or lecturers teach; and learn also how to socialise with other people.

Memorising facts does not help one to think. Education is organised thought developed in the subconscious and built on consciousness.

Why do you sleep? I don't know about you, but my reasons for sleeping are: o   I can't stay awake for twenty-four hours

- To rest
- To allow my body to shut down and recharge fully
- To be able to function properly Sleep is an active period in which a lot of important processing, restoration, and strengthening occurs. Exactly how this happens and why our bodies are programmed for such a long period of slumber is still somewhat of a mystery. But scientists understand some of sleep's critical functions, and the reasons we need it for optimal health and wellbeing. One of the vital roles of sleep is to help us solidify and consolidate memories. As we go about our day, our brains take in an incredible amount of information. Research shows that after people sleep, they tend to retain information and perform better on memory tasks. Our bodies all require long periods of sleep in order to restore and rejuvenate, to grow muscle, repair tissue, and synthesise hormones.

Why do you get into a romantic relationship? Be honest. Is it because: o   Of loneliness?

- You love the specific person? o You need money?
- You need someone to tell you he/she loves you?

Starting a relationship is a big decision, so it's a good idea first to know why you want it. Are you ready for the give-and-take of sharing, or are you simply feeling lonely?

Are you emotionally ready now, or would you be better off waiting? There's no need to rush; take the time to think it through. Wanting to be with someone, to have someone to care for and share things with, is all part of developing as a person. But it's okay to take your time and to wait until you genuinely feel you're ready to be in a relationship. Here are some ways to tell that you're ready:

- You're comfortable with who you are
- It's something you want, not something you feel you should have o   You're willing to wait for the right person
- You're ready to give your time and attention to someone else o You aren't being pressured into a relationship by others

If you're not sure that you're ready for a relationship, take a breather and don't rush into anything serious. And if you think you are ready, then wait for the right person to come along.

Why do you drink water? I have to admit that I make a point of drinking eight glasses of water a day:

- Because I am thirsty
- Because experts say it's good to drink water o   To allow my body and brain to function well

Humans need to drink water to survive. Your body is approximately 60 percent water, your brain is 70% water, and your lungs are nearly 90% water. Each day, your body must replace about 2.4 litres of water through ingested liquid and foods. Your body uses water in many ways.

Drinking water helps maintain the balance of body fluids. The functions of these bodily fluids include digestion, absorption, circulation, creation of saliva, transportation of nutrients, and maintenance of body temperature. Water cushions and lubricates joints; nourishes and protects the brain, spinal cord and other tissues; keeps the body's temperature normal; and helps remove waste through perspiration, bowel movements and urination.

Seeing that you are reading this book, I assume that you're in the habit of reading (which is a wonderfully beneficial habit to have, by the way). But have you wondered about the reasons why you read? I read to:
- Get information
- Have fun
- Improve my knowledge about the world and things
- Learn from others so I can improve my own life in an efficient way

Books teach us how to think, how to relate to people, what to do, who we are and who we should be. For the most part, they teach us how to live. And as American author EE Cummings put it, nothing is as difficult as that. I have yet to meet anyone who does not flounder when it comes to figuring out what they want to do with their lives. Or who they are. Or who they want to be. We all need guidance and books have a unique knack for providing it.

Books enable us to garner more experience and knowledge than it would be possible to accumulate in a lifetime. We can learn from the mistakes and successes of others, applying their wisdom to our lives.

As William Somerset Maugham, highest-paid British author during the 1930s wrote: "To acquire the habit of reading is to construct for yourself a refuge from almost all the miseries of life."

Why do you go to work every day? Is it: o   To pay the bills?

- To be creditworthy?
- Because everybody goes there?
- To discover your talents and become a better person?

You go to work to make money. Make money to do what? Do you want a certain lifestyle? What type of a lifestyle? Do you want to fulfil your family's needs? What are those needs? Do you want to have a home and a car and to take vacations? What kind of a home, car and vacation? We can go on and on.

The bottom line is that you go to work to fulfil your needs. However, you have probably met your basic needs, and you are really going to work to fulfil your dreams, as each of us has different dreams and desires.
Once you realise this, then work is nothing but a stepping stone to help you get where you want to go. The real problem is: do you know where you want to go?

What are your dreams? Do you know where you want to be, what you want to do or to have in three, five, ten or even twenty years? Please remember, work is nothing but a stepping stone to help you get where you want to go.

First, decide where you want to go, what is the long-term dream, and assess how you can use your job to get to your desired destination. When your job and your dream are connected, you get more excited about going to work. You are more motivated, and you will realise your dream.

To do better in the future, it's essential for you to discover why you do what you do; discover what your reasons are. Don't live like a robot that is only able to follow its programme. You have the power of reason, use it. If what you are doing at present is not working, change it. If your power switch is off, turn it on. It's time to raise the bar.

Flip that switch
Action Steps

➢ **Step 1**

Think about the reasons why you do things like eating, sleeping, working, praying, procrastinating, exercising, remaining in a relationship or abstaining from a relationship:

➢ **Step 2**

Are there things you'd like to change? Write them down and specify how, when and why you intend changing them:

A note on switching on your power

"I will never apologise for being me. You should apologise for asking me to be anything else but me."
– Anonymous

I hope you enjoy reading this book as much as I enjoyed writing it. I urge you to become the best you can be and to switch on your power.

Switching on your power is not about going on an ego trip. It's not about being better than others. It's definitely not about trampling on others so that you can be on top!

I urge you to switch on your power so that you become the best person you can be and live life to the fullest. Because being the best you is beneficial to yourself and to the people who interact with you regularly, and it gives due glory to your Creator. As Rick Warren points out in his best-selling book, 'What on Earth Am I Here For?', you could reach all your personal goals, become a raving success by the world's standards and still miss the purpose for which God created you.

Respect yourself enough to walk away from anything that no longer serves you, grows you or makes you happy. Respect starts with self; it's an inside- out process. When last did you walk away from thoughts that were no longer serving you? From beliefs that were toxic to your being? Your identity that was misaligned with your dreams and desires?

When last did you walk away from the habits that stole your time and peace of mind? From eating unhealthy food that harms your body?
Walked away from procrastination and excuse-making? Walked away from bad company and refused to stoop to their level? Walked away from grudges, regardless of how badly people treated you?

Let today be the day that you walk away from serious flaws, and undesirable obstacles and people. Let today be the day that you give mouth-to-mouth resuscitation to your forgotten dreams and skills. Let today be the day that you step away from the darkness into the light, the day you switch on your power!

Acknowledgements

Firstly I would like to thank God, the Almighty for revealing my life's purpose through the scripture found in Matthew 7:7-8 King James Version (KJV): "Ask, and it shall be given you; seek, and ye shall find; knock, and it shall be opened unto you:

For every one that asketh receiveth; and he that seeketh findeth; and to him that knocketh it shall be opened."
The above scripture helped me realise the gifts, talents and abilities known to me now that were lying dormant. All I had to do was ask, seek and knock; lo and behold they were revealed to me.

I have truly been lucky and blessed to have come into contact with all kinds of people from all walks of life, who wittingly or unwittingly allowed me the honour and privilege to form and shape my opinions on what matters in life. To all those men and women of substance, reason, compassion, conscience, conviction, courage and goodwill – thank you so very much, for embracing me as one of your own.

My family: My wife Mpumi Ndaba and our two lovely boys Ntokozo and Sanele Ndaba who believe in me and stand by me no matter how wild the dream. My late mom Ellen Ntombini Ndaba and my great aunt Catherine Thembani Nkosi, who made me the man I am and taught me about humility and love. My late brother Sydney Ndaba, my sister Deborah Ndaba, and my brother Joshua Ndaba.

Friends and associates: Gordon Rolls, James Mpele, Alfred'Ali' Zimu, Dominic Gaobepe and Dr Phil Pinga.

The professional team behind this book: Eulália Snyman and Dylan Fourie. My mentors: I would like to acknowledge all the mentors (in-person and virtual) in my life who have really left their mark. These mentors (awesome men and women of the world) have mainly been virtual – via books, videos and blogs, hence I can't single out just a few.

All the people that have made a contribution and have helped to shape the person I have become, thank you, thank you! I thank everyone from the bottom of my heart.

To you reading this book – thank you and best wishes.

Veli Ndaba – 'The Engineered Mind – to WIN' 2018

References and suggested reading

You Are Born to Win – by Veli Ndaba
Your Dream is Calling You – by Veli Ndaba
Deep Work– by Dr Cal Newport
The Power of Habit: Why we Do What we Do in Life and Business – by Charles Duhigg
Your Daily W.O.W – by Melissa West
How to Win Friends and Influence People – By Dale Carnegie
Man's Search for Meaning – by Viktor Frankl
The Holy Bible
Awaken the Giant Within – by Tony Robbins
What They Won't Teach You in School – by Jossy Jonacs
The Art of Exceptional Living – by Jim Rohn
In Search of Excellence – by Thomas J. Peters and Robert H. Waterman, Jr.
Long Walk to Freedom – by Nelson Mandela
It's Not Over Until You Win: How to become the person you always wanted to be no matter what the obstacle – by Les Brown
Your Erroneous Zone – by Dr Wayne Dyer
Getting Started With Neurofeedback – by John N. Demos
Snakes in Suits: When Psychopaths Go to Work – by Paul Babiak and Robert Hare
What on Earth Am I here For? – by Rick Warren
Success Secrets – by Mark H. McCormack
The 10X Rule – by Grant Cardone
From the Streets of Soweto to Soccer Superstar – by Lucas Radebe

I asked God – a prayer answered
Author unknown

I asked God for STRENGTH
and God gave me difficulties to make me strong!
I prayed for WISDOM
and God gave me problems to learn to solve!
I asked God for PROSPERITY
and God gave me brains and strength to work!
I prayed for COURAGE
and God gave me dangers to overcome!
I asked for LOVE
and God gave me troubled people to help!
I prayed for FAVOURS
and God gave me opportunities!
I asked for HUMILITY
and God gave me experiences not to be proud!
I asked God to grant me PATIENCE and God said "NO"
He said that patience is a by-product of tribulation; it isn't
granted, it's earned.
I asked God to spare me PAIN and God said "NO"
He said suffering draws you apart from worldly cares and
brings you closer to Me!
I received nothing I wanted...
I received everything I needed... My prayer has been
answered... **AMEN**

www.ingramcontent.com/pod-product-compliance
Lightning Source LLC
Chambersburg PA
CBHW021232090426
42740CB00006B/490